Flora Thompson:
Beyond Candleford

Flora Jane Thompson was born (née Timms) in 1876 at Juniper Hill on the Oxfordshire/Northamptonshire border. She started work in a neighbouring post office at the age of fourteen, thus beginning a long connection with the Post Office. At the age of twenty-one, she took a position as sub-office assistant to the postmaster in Grayshott, Hampshire (her *Heatherley*), and was to stay in Hampshire for the next thirty years of her life. After leaving Grayshott she married John Thompson in January 1903 and moved to Bournemouth. Their daughter Winifred (called Diana) was born in October of that year, and their first son Basil in 1909. In 1916, a month after Flora's favourite brother Edwin was killed in action in Belgium, John Thompson applied for the position of postmaster at Liphook (her *Peverel*).

The family thus moved back to within three miles of Grayshott, and Flora was able to renew her acquaintance with the area. Easier times followed the end of the First World War and, despite the arrival of a third child, Peter, in 1918, Flora began writing more industriously during this period than at any other time. Here she wrote her nature notes, *The Peverel Papers*, from her own observations during her long and frequent walks in the area, and here in 1926 the family bought a house of their own for the first time, having previously been forced to live in rented Post Office accommodation. But hardly had they settled in than John Thompson applied for promotion again and moved to Dartmouth in November 1927. Flora stayed in her beloved Liphook for nearly a year more while the house was sold, and then followed, never to return to Hampshire.

During the next ten years she revised some of the notes she had written about her early childhood and developed them into the book *Lark Rise* which was to bring her fame late in life. The success of this book led to the publication of two more, and their eventual appearance as the trilogy *Lark Rise to Candleford*. She wrote a fourth book, *Heatherley*, a sequel following on from *Candleford Green* and telling of her time in Grayshott, but chose not to publish it. Instead, she wrote *Still Glides the Stream* — her final publication.

Flora Thompson died at Brixham, Devon, on 21st May 1947.

Flora Thompson:
Beyond Candleford

Comprising two plays

Flora's Heatherley

and

Flora's Peverel

John Owen Smith

Flora Thompson: Beyond Candleford
First published 1996, as *Flora's Heatherley* and *Flora's Peverel*
This combined edition published 2011

Typeset and published by John Owen Smith
19 Kay Crescent, Headley Down, Hampshire GU35 8AH

Tel: 01428 712892
wordsmith@johnowensmith.co.uk
www.johnowensmith.co.uk

For further plays by the same author see www.johnowensmith.co.uk

ISBN 978-1-873855-63-8

Printed and bound in Great Britain by CPI Antony Rowe, Chippenham and
Eastbourne

Introduction

When by some mischance I started to research the history of Headley, where I live, on the Hampshire/Surrey border, I was told that one of the postmistresses here at the end of the nineteenth century had gone on to become quite famous.

That was my first introduction to Flora Thompson who, to my shame, I hadn't heard of until that moment.

She is, of course, known to most people as the author of *Lark Rise to Candleford*, which tells of her childhood in Oxfordshire; but my interest lay in her life in Hampshire during which she developed the skills to write her celebrated work in later life. And her journey was not an easy one.

I decided to investigate. My prime sources of information were her published works connected with east Hampshire, *Heatherley* and the *Peverel Papers*; the book *Grayshott* written by the late J H (Jack) Smith; the various historical booklets published over several years by the Bramshott & Liphook Preservation Society; the biography *Flora Thompson* by Gillian Lindsay; and *The Hilltop Writers* written by W R (Bob) Trotter.

But, naturally enough, the most exciting sources were the unexpected and unpublished ones, those that came from ferreting through various public and private archives, hunting for clues, tracking down descendants and others who might have anything to add to the story; writing, phoning, visiting, recording, and finally piecing the jigsaw puzzle together.

The process was enjoyable, and in so many interesting ways the story which emerged was not entirely the one as told by Flora.

I published the results in my book *On the Trail of Flora Thompson* in 1997. Then, having been asked to write a community play for local theatrical groups to perform, I decided to give Flora's local story an outing on the stage.

In fact it received two outings, as I chose to split her Grayshott and Liphook stories into two separate plays: *Flora's Heatherley* and *Flora's Peverel*. In this, I followed the lead of Keith Dewhurst who in the late 1970s had written two plays based on *Lark Rise to Candleford*, but whereas he was dramatising a book, I was dramatising a life and this posed problems when Flora's literary personalities differed from the real-life ones.

First and most obviously was her well-known use of pseudonyms. She names herself 'Laura' in her book *Heatherley*, as she does in *Lark Rise to Candleford*, but I chose to call her Flora in the plays. With other characters the decision was more difficult. I knew her young assistant, whom she calls 'Alma Stedman', was really Annie Symonds and that is who we meet in the play. Likewise her unfortunate employer in Grayshott was Walter Chapman and not 'Mr Hertford' as she calls him. But with other characters the choice was not so easy. I am 99% certain that the boyfriend she calls Richard Brownlow was actually a William Elwes – but that 1% of doubt stopped me from naming him as such in the plays.

In *Flora's Peverel* I was less constrained by pseudonyms, as this play was largely based on historical research rather than Flora's own work, but since it covered a more recent period I found myself dramatising the lives of people who were still alive. At the first performance an 86-year-old Eileen Leggett was in the audience watching herself being portrayed at age 16 on the stage. Fortunately she had been one of my sources of information, and I had taken the wise precaution of clearing that bit of the script with her first!

John Owen Smith
Headley Down
January 2011

In order to help directors with their interpretation of the characters, as well as for general interest, I have added as appendices an abridged timeline of Flora's life, a potted history of the people represented in the plays and a discussion of staging issues.

Flora's Peverel was first performed as the opening production in the new theatre complex at Bedales School near Petersfield on 20th May 1997, the day before the 50th anniversary of Flora's death, and then toured other locations in the east Hampshire/west Surrey area.

Flora's Heatherley was first performed at the Grayshott Literary Festival in September 1998, exactly a century after Flora had first walked into the village. It also toured other locations in the area.

Flora's Heatherley

First part of 'Flora Thompson: Beyond Candleford'

Flora Thompson in Grayshott 1898–1901

Flora came to Grayshott (her "Heatherley") in 1898 at the age of 21 to take the position of sub-postoffice assistant, and stayed for two and a half years. She arrived as a young, gauche, country girl, and passed "from foolish youth to wicked adolescence" in the village.

The theme of the play is essentially about the conventions of the period, particularly with respect to courtship and marriage, and Flora's difficulty in conforming to them.

She drew disapproval by associating with 'strange' men, and walking for miles alone on the surrounding heaths, and felt more at home having tea with a retired 'big-game' hunter, or learning about local wildlife from a cowman on the common, than walking decorously up and down the village street with the other village girls.

Meanwhile she could no longer stand the quarrels between the postmaster and his wife, and found lodgings on her own for the first time in her life. [Two years later he murdered his wife and was diagnosed as criminally insane]. At the same time, her beloved brother volunteered to fight in the Boer War, and she looked with concern for his name every time she posted up the latest news.

She came in contact with the literary 'greats' who lived locally at the time: Arthur Conan Doyle, George Bernard Shaw, Richard le Gallienne and Grant Allen all used her post office. The immediate effect was to cause her to destroy all her writings up to that time, thinking she could never compete— but it almost certainly encouraged her writing career in the long run.

During her last year in 'Heatherley' she met the man she calls 'Richard Brownlow.' He came close to proposing to her, but in the end she left the village still a single girl. She married another post office worker, John, less than two years later—and at the end of the play we anticipate the effect this is to have on the 'free spirit' we observed in 'Heatherley'. He will become the 'dodder' in her life.

Note: Since this play was written it has been recognised that Flora probably left Grayshott at some time in the year 1900 rather than in 1901. However in 'Heatherley' she mentions the effect of Queen Victoria's death (January 1901) on the villagers, so we have retained this date for Act 2.

The second play, "Flora's Peverel," covers Flora's life in Liphook from 1916–28 as a married woman with children of her own.

Flora's Heatherley

Act 1 – 1899

Scene 1: Inside the Chapmans' accommodation at Grayshott Post Office, 1899

Scene 2: In Grayshott Post Office, next morning

Scene 3: At the site of the proposed Refreshment House, Grayshott

Scene 4: In Grayshott Post Office, some weeks later

Scene 5: On Ludshott Common, later that day

Scene 6: A Sunday afternoon in Crossways Road, Grayshott

Scene 7: In Grayshott Post Office, a few days later

Scene 8: Inside the Chapmans' accommodation at Grayshott Post Office, that night

Scene 9: In Grayshott Post Office, a few days later

Scene 10: In Crossways Road, Grayshott, soon after

Scene 11: In Mr Foreshaw's House, next Sunday afternoon

Scene 12: In Crossways Road, Grayshott, a Sunday afternoon some weeks later

Scene 13: The opening of the Fox & Pelican, Grayshott

Scene 14: In Grayshott Post Office, a few days later

— INTERVAL —

Act 2 – 1901

Scene 15: In Grayshott Post Office, 1901

Scene 16: In the Chapmans' accommodation at Grayshott Post Office

Scene 17: At Flora's lodgings with Mrs Parkhurst

Scene 18: Sir Frederick Pollock meets with Conan Doyle

Scene 19: In Grayshott Post Office soon after

Scene 20: On Ludshott Common soon after

Scene 21: In Crossways Road, Grayshott

Scene 22: Mrs Parkhurst's house, some weeks later

Scene 23: In Grayshott Post Office, some time later

Scene 24: In Crossways Road, immediately after

Scene 25: In Grayshott Post Office, at the same time

Scene 26: In Crossways Road, Grayshott, some time later
Scene 27: By the new Hindhead Telegraph Office
Scene 28: Mrs Parkhurst's house, some days later
Scene 29: In Grayshott Post Office, a few days later
Scene 30: Farewells in Grayshott
Scene 31: Inside the Chapmans' accommodation at Grayshott Post Office
Scene 32: Epilogue
Scene 33: Flora's Wedding, 7th January 1903, at Twickenham

Cast (ages in 1899)
Walter Chapman (43)
Emily Chapman (36)
Annie Symonds (20)
Flora Timms (22)
Charles Foreshaw (an old 62)
Sir Frederick Pollock (54)
George Bernard Shaw (43)
Marion (21)
Bob Pikesley (an old 40)
Isobel ('Izzy') – (20)
Winifred Storr (13)
Grace ('Gee') Leuchars (14)
Arthur Conan Doyle (40)
Ernest Chapman (41)
Richard Brownlow (22)
Mavis Brownlow (20)
Mrs Parkhurst (an old 45)
Mrs Davidson (say 50)
William Sillick, reporter (21)
Man in the Pub
Alfred & Willie, telegram boys
John Thompson – *non-speaking*
Flora as a Bride – *non-speaking*

Flora's Heatherley

Scene 1

Inside the Chapmans' accommodation at Grayshott Post Office, 1899

Offstage we hear a commotion

Walter Chapman *(Shouting)* Enjoyed it, did you? Left me here on my own and enjoyed yourself!

Emily Chapman But you said I could go—you gave me the ticket.

Walter Chapman *(Entering)* A piano recital! A two guinea ticket to a piano recital!

Emily Chapman *(Follows)* The ticket was free—complimentary—for the post office.

Walter Chapman I am the postmaster here, not you.

Emily Chapman But you said …

Walter Chapman You know he lies in wait for me. *(Hissing under his breath)* To be or not to be.

Emily Chapman Nobody lies in wait for you, Walter.

Walter Chapman Imagine it, do I? *(Hissing)* Vengeance is mine, saith the Lord.

Emily Chapman Walter …

Walter Chapman He thinks he'll get me, but I'll get him first! *(He has a headache)* My head!

Emily Chapman There's no-one.

Walter Chapman Or perhaps it's that girl—perhaps she's been sent by him.

Emily Chapman Not Flora!

Walter Chapman Miss Timms—yes, perhaps it's her. She'll let him in while I'm asleep—he'll murder us in our beds!

Emily Chapman She'll hear us—she's only in the next room.

Walter Chapman But I have my revolver ready.

Emily Chapman Walter, you must see a doctor—be reasonable.

Walter Chapman *(Reacting angrily)* A doctor? A doctor, Mrs Chapman? And what do you think a doctor can do for me, eh? My heart is buried in poor Letty's grave! Can Dr Lyndon bring her back?

Emily Chapman She has been dead for over twenty years!

Walter Chapman You are in her place—her place! She would not have left me tonight.

Emily Chapman We have three children now—ours—yours and mine—do they mean nothing to you?

Walter Chapman Her picture's still on my bedroom wall—she would not have left me. *(Incoherent)* Why did you leave me, Letty?

Emily Chapman Walter!

Walter Chapman *(Turning on Emily)* And now I have to live with you!

Emily Chapman Walter, no!

Walter Chapman You and your immorality!

Emily Chapman *(Getting hysterical)* No!

Walter Chapman *(Hissing)* Vengeance is mine …

Emily Chapman No, Walter! No!

Walter Chapman … I will repay, saith the Lord.

Emily Chapman *(Running off, weeping)* No! No! No!

Walter Chapman *(Following her, shouting)* I will repay, saith the Lord!

Scene 2

In Grayshott Post Office, next morning

Flora and Annie are at work behind the counter

Annie You're brooding again, Flora.

Flora I'm sorry, Annie. *(Smiling for her)* Is that better?

Annie Yes. You think too much, you know, that's your trouble.

Flora I'm older than you.

Annie Only by two years! Were they arguing again last night?

Flora Yes.

Annie It gets you down, doesn't it?

Flora I have to live in the same house.

Annie They're just a typical married couple—always falling in and falling out with each other.

Flora I think it's a bit more serious than that.

Annie There you are—thinking again! They've different temperaments, that's all. Stands to reason they'll tiff from time to time.

Flora You don't have to listen to it every evening.

Annie Cheer up! *(Sorting the mail)* Ly-ces-ter, War-ces-ter, Has-le-merry—isn't English a funny language!

Flora But he'll come out here today to meet his trade customers as if nothing's happened.

Annie There you are then. *(Still sorting)* Look, this ones going to Bucking-ham—isn't that near where you come from?

Flora Yes, my Uncle Tom lives there. I wonder who's writing …

The telegraph machine starts to tinkle out its message

Annie Telegraph coming! Shall I take it down this time?

Flora The sooner you learn, the sooner I can have some half days off.

Annie All I need is practice.

Flora I'll listen to it from here and see if you get it right.

Annie *(Going off to the machine)* I only got two letters wrong last time.

The telegraph machine continues its message

Annie FORESHAW—it's for Mr Foreshaw.

Flora Concentrate, or you'll miss the rest of it.

As the machine tinkles on, an old gentleman enters. It is Mr Foreshaw, though Flora does not know him—he has some envelopes in his arthritic hands.

Foreshaw Some stamps for these letters, if you please.

Flora Certainly, sir. *(She removes the stamps from her ledger book)* Three letters—that's thruppence please. *(Takes the money and hands the stamps to him)* Thank you—your stamps.

She can see that he has difficulty in sticking them on

Foreshaw Hands aren't all they used to be, I'm afraid.

Flora Here, let me help—I'll stick them on for you. *(She takes them back and starts to do so)*

Foreshaw Against post office rules, you know. Get you into trouble.

Flora I don't think the Postmaster-General is looking.

By this time the tinkling of the telegraph machine has stopped, and Annie returns

Annie Here we are—I think it makes sense. Oh, Mr Foreshaw, you're here!

Flora You are Mr Foreshaw?

Foreshaw I am.

Annie There's a telegram just arrived for you.

Foreshaw Indeed. What does it say?

Annie hands the message to him

Thank you. *(He reads it)* Huh, I see. Yes. I see. Well. Thank you—good day to you then. *(He turns and exits)*

Flora He was a bit gruff.

Annie Oh, don't worry about him—he's known to be a woman-hater.

Flora Is he indeed? Why should that be?

Annie I don't know. It's said he won't have a woman in the house. Did I get the message right?

Flora I hope so—you forgot to show it to me!

Annie He had a bungalow built for himself two or three years ago at the end of a long track. He lives there on his own.

Flora Poor old man.

Annie Why 'poor old man'?—I expect he enjoys being alone. Anyway, you're a fine one to talk. You go walking for miles across the commons on your own.

Flora I'm not sure I'd like to *live* on my own though.

Annie Don't worry, Mr Right will come along for you one day, then you'll be all right. *(Laughs at the pun)* Men prefer a quiet sort like you for a wife.

Flora For a wife? *I* shan't get married.

Annie Course you will. It's only natural for a woman—my mother says.

Flora Not for me.

Annie You just wait, he'll come along—and when he says 'snip' you'll say 'snap' fast enough.

Flora *(Laughing)* Annie, what a thing! Is that what your mother says too?

Annie Yes, and she's right. You wait and see.

Walter Chapman has entered silently and stands behind Flora. She turns round suddenly and is startled to see him there. As she reacts, he throws back his head and goes through a 'pantomime of hilarious laughter' without uttering a sound.

Flora Mr Chapman, you startled me!

Walter Chapman Just checking everything is all right, Miss Timms—just checking.

Flora Everything is fine, thank you.

Walter Chapman And Miss Symonds?

Annie No problems at all, Mr Chapman.

Walter Chapman Good. Good. Then I shall return to my carpentry. We must all earn our living. *(He turns to exit, then looks back)* You have not seen *Mrs* Chapman recently?

Flora I'm afraid not.

Walter Chapman It matters not, it matters not. *(He exits)*

Annie I expect she's walked out on him again.

Flora Is that saying 'snap' when he says 'snip'?

Annie Oh, she'll come back—she always does. Like I say, just a tiff. *(Looking out of the window)* Now what's going on out there?

Flora Where?

Annie By the crossroads. That writer with the red beard's there—still on his crutch. They say he fell off a bicycle.

Flora Mr Bernard Shaw.

Annie You know him?

Flora Only by name—from the letters addressed to him.

Annie I thought he might be one of those strange men you're always talking to on your walks.

Flora *(Bruised)* Annie!

Annie You're getting a reputation you know. Much safer to stick with us girls. Oh look, there's Sir Frederick Pollock with him. Must be about the new pub.

Flora Refreshment House you mean.

Annie Refreshment House! Can you see that idea working in Grayshott? Can you see old Alfie Wells drinking mineral water?

Flora Who?

Annie Alfie, the blacksmith. Works in a shower of sparks and swear-words. They'll get no trade from the likes of him if they don't sell beer.

Flora I think they mean to sell it, but not at a profit.

Annie Sounds silly to me. It won't work here, mark my words.

Scene 3

At the site of the proposed Refreshment House, Grayshott

George Bernard Shaw, on a crutch, talks with Sir Frederick Pollock

Pollock We have the licence, Mr Shaw. Our Grayshott & District Refreshment Association may now proceed with its plans.

Shaw There'll be opposition of course. Lady Mary Murray down in Tilford told me we were deliberately opening a centre for crime and demoralisation.

Pollock She's a daughter of Lord Carlisle—what do you expect from the Liberal-Temperance press?

Shaw I suggested that perhaps she'd prefer the Alton brewers to build a public house here instead, for that was the likely alternative.

Pollock I imagine she was not persuaded by the argument.

Shaw She was not either. We intend to stock alcoholic drinks, and that's cause enough for her to condemn us—no matter that we shall also supply the community with tea, coffee and good nourishing food.

Pollock And the manager will receive his commission from the sale of those, not on the sale of alcohol.

Shaw So I told her.

Pollock It's an experiment which has succeeded elsewhere. It has the blessing of the Archbishop of Canterbury, no less.

Shaw And deserves the hearty sympathy of all those with *intelligence* who are on the side of temperance in the village—whether they drink or not.

Pollock But does it not offend your Socialist principles, Mr Shaw? We may perhaps stand accused of denying the working man his natural environment.

Shaw The inhabitants of Hindhead and Grayshott, Sir Frederick, have insisted on my lecturing to them constantly since I arrived here, and will hear of no other subject than Socialism. Personally, I have come just to get some rest from Socialist propaganda and to recover my broken health.

Pollock Point taken, point taken. But Socialism is not your only subject. I gather at one of your meetings you recently *'cured Conan Doyle of sentimental pacifism and left him a raging Jingo!'*, as someone put it.

Shaw That was just up the road in the Congregational Hall. He was in the chair, and we had a very lively discussion on European Disarmament. You should have come along.

Pollock I'll no doubt read the reports in the press.

Shaw We were not far from Doyle's new house there, of course. *Under-shaw*—did you ever hear such an awful pun in naming a house!

Pollock Pun?

Shaw People are saying he called it that just because I live a bit up the hill from him.

Pollock He tells me his 'shaw' is an Anglo-Saxon word meaning 'grove of trees.' But perhaps you should be flattered. He could equally have called it *Underrussell* or even *Underpollock* I suppose.

Shaw That would be taking a pun too far. In years to come, people here will wonder at the strange clutch of characters who came to inhabit their hill top.

Pollock I think they already do. How many of them, I wonder, really understand these speeches of yours. Socialism—Pacifism—Vegetarianism—Disestablishmentarianism …

Shaw That's the talk of a feudal lord!—insulting their intelligence.

Pollock Intelligence, no. But the district seems to have become some sort of literary ghetto in recent years—authors of all sorts and styles here—and pretty confusing for the average person, I think.

Shaw Well I intend to donate a small library of books to this Refreshment House when it opens—to extend the mind as well as the body of your average person.

Pollock Something from our local authors?

Shaw Probably not—the customers will have heard enough of them. One of Tolstoy's later works perhaps, some of Kipling's short stories, an illustrated George Du Maurier …

Pollock And no doubt some learnèd tracts on Socialism, Temperance and the rest?

Shaw *(Chuckling)* That's a possibility, Sir Frederick, a possibility.

Scene 4

In Grayshott Post Office, some weeks later

Marion enters the shop—she is a moon-faced girl in her early twenties,
and is flustered

Marion Flora, I need your help.

Flora Why, Marion, shouldn't you be in your sweet shop? What's all this?

Marion It's for the Christian Endeavour movement. You know we have a guest speaker each Thursday evening at the chapel.

Flora I remember you telling me—it's your job to put the glass of water on the table for them.

Marion Yes—but the new pastor has decided we members should take it in turns to speak ourselves, *instead* of having a guest.

Flora And by the look on your face, Marion, I'd say you've just found out it's your turn soon.

Marion In a fortnight! Flora, what shall I talk about? I've never done anything like this before.

Flora Does it have to be a religious subject?

Marion Not always, but it has to be serious. Do you think *'Total Abstinence versus Moderation'* would do? I heard an excellent address on that at a Band of Hope meeting once—I think I can remember most of it.

Flora The village might be a bit weary of that topic at the moment. Try something that's new to them. Something you know more about than they do.

Marion But what? My mind's a complete blank.

Flora Well, let's think then—how about as a title, 'The Sweets of Life'? You could tell them some of your experiences in the sweet shop as a little light relief, then go on and draw the moral that the best things in life actually cost nothing.

Marion *(Her eyes opened)* Flora, that's wonderful! How do you come up with these ideas? Oh, that's such a relief!

Flora Now all you have to do is write it.

Marion Write it—yes.

Flora In a fortnight.

Marion Yes. I'll start now—well, as soon as the shop shuts. Oh, you've taken a weight off my mind, Flora, I don't mind telling you. I don't know how you do it, I really don't. I'll bring you in a bag of fruit drops next time I come. *(She exits gleefully to the street)*

Annie enters from inside the post office

Annie Was that sweet Marion?

Flora After ideas for a speech to the chapel.

Annie Marion, make a speech? Good heavens, I can't imagine it—she's not the type.

Flora I gave her the first title that came into my head, and she's thrilled with it. I don't think we've seen the last of her though.

Annie Nor do I. She'll be asking you to write it next.

Flora If I write anything in my spare time, it won't be speeches to the Christian Endeavour movement.

Annie What will it be then?

Flora I don't know. I've been a great 'spoiler of paper,' as my mother put it, in the past—but somehow, here in Grayshott …

Annie It's the ideal place to write. There's famous authors all around us.

Flora Yes. But seeing them here has made me ashamed of all my old efforts. In fact I put a match to some of them the other night.

Annie Flora! How could you? All that work gone.

Flora It was nothing much. A journal I was keeping and a few other scraps. They'll not be missed. *(More brightly)* Anyway, now you're back I can be on my way—my shift ended five minutes ago. *(She starts getting ready to leave)*

Annie Yes. I don't normally see you for dust—out of that door quick as a flash you are, usually. Got a secret admirer somewhere, have you?

Flora You know I haven't.

Annie *(Only half jokingly)* I'm not so sure. You're a deep one, you are. Where are you off to this time, then? Meeting Bob Pikesley in the middle of nowhere again?

Flora I wish I hadn't mentioned him to you now—we were only sheltering from a storm together.

Annie *(Laughing)* Tell *that* to the curate!

Flora Anyway, I'm off down to Waggoners Wells today—nowhere near Bob Pikesley's place.

Annie Right past old Boddy Hill the broomsquire's though. Tongues will wag.

Flora *(Ready to go)* Let them wag. I just want to enjoy God's good air in my own good company.

Annie *(Rather primly)* See you tomorrow, then. Enjoy yourself—and your own good company.

Flora exits quickly into the street as Annie gets on with her work

Flora *(To herself)* Why does everyone have to so interested in other people's affairs? If you're not seen to be doing the right thing, and on your way to getting decently married, you never hear the last of it. *(She walks off)*

Walter Chapman has entered silently and stands behind Annie
—she senses him and jumps

Walter Chapman I'm just seeing if Mr Vertue has arrived.

Annie N-no, sir, he hasn't. But I'm told your brother was looking for you earlier.

Walter Chapman My brother Ernest is not important. He would only want to talk religion and reconciliation to me. Mr Vertue is coming to discuss business.

Annie Yes, sir.

Walter Chapman If you see him, you will let me know.

Annie I will, sir.

Walter Chapman Thank you. *(Hissing)* 'Now is the winter of our discontent.'

Annie Our what?

Walter Chapman No matter. It is some carving he wants me to do—for his private chapel.

Annie *(Dubiously)* I see.

Walter Chapman I shall go back and sharpen my tools—in preparation. Dangerous to use blunt tools on a job, you know.

Walter exits into the house as the lights fade on the scene

Scene 5

On Ludshott Common, later that day

Flora out walking, observing nature as she goes,
almost walks into Bob Pikesley

Bob Pikesley A'ternoon.

Flora *(Startled)* Oh, Bob. Good afternoon. You're a long way from home.

Bob Pikesley Few miles—no distance at all. *(Pause)* Weather's on the turn.

Flora Is it? I thought it looked quite settled.

Bob Pikesley Be rain afore you get home.

Flora I don't mind the rain. At least, not unless it's too heavy.

Bob Pikesley It'll be heavy.

Flora You think so?

Bob Pikesley Like last time.

Flora Well there's plenty of cover here if I need it—and I'll remember what you told me, about not sitting on wet pine needles.

Bob Pikesley Helpless crittur you were to be sure. There's always a dry seat under pines in any weather.

Flora I know—I remember. Just brush the top inch of needles aside …

Bob Pikesley Then sit down, lean your back against the trunk, and you'll have a seat fit for a queen.

Flora Warm and dry.

Bob Pikesley Aye, warm and dry. That's more than I'd wish for that dressed up, la-di-da young devil who visited me the other day though.

Flora Who?

Bob Pikesley A sanitary inspector, he called himself. Came from God knows where and told me to dig a 'proper well' as he called it, or I couldn't sell no more milk. He said my spring was polluted. Eighty pounds that'll cost me, according to 'Dumpy' Winchester.

Flora That's hard lines.

Bob Pikesley Hard lines? Put me in debt for the rest of my life, it will. Just sent here by the devil to make me sink that well, he was. Not interfering with nobody else as I hears of.

Flora People are getting very germ-conscious now.

Bob Pikesley He's only here for a short while, too. He'll be gone by the time the well's dug. I'd well him if I had my way—put him down the thing and make him stay there!

Flora *(Changing the subject)* You say you know this common like the back of your hand.

Bob Pikesley Aye, and every flower, bird and beast upon it.

Flora They tell me there's adders here, but I've never seen one.

Bob Pikesley You never have? They're all around you. Look—watch you here. But be quiet now.

He beckons her to follow him, and they creep to one side.
He puts a finger to his lips to keep her silent, and points into the undergrowth

Bob Pikesley *(Whispering)* There—do you see? Coming out of the heather and onto the path.

Flora How did you … ?

Bob Pikesley *(Motioning her to keep quiet)* See them marks? They're Vs— V's for viper. Never you touch a snake with them marks on it. There— now he's gone.

Flora How did you know it was there?

Bob Pikesley I saw the heather over there moving in sort of waves, so I knew a snake of some sort were coming our way. Shrews and mice don't make it move like that. Now grass snakes like cooler places, and slow worms don't make much stir when they move, so stands to reason it was an adder.

Flora I'm glad you didn't kill it.

Bob Pikesley They don't hurt me, so why should I hurt them? Unless I find one near my cowshed, of course. Now that reminds me—you'll be passing my cottage on your way home.

Flora Yes, I can go that way.

Bob Pikesley Then take a message to my sister. I'll be a while on the heath yet, so she'd better do the cows tonight. You'll remember to tell her that, will you?

Flora I'll remember that, Bob.

Bob Pikesley Well, run along then.

Flora feels reluctant to be ordered around, a bit like a child, and lingers

Go on with you! And mind the snakes! *(To himself as she exits)* Helpless young crittur!

Scene 6

A Sunday afternoon in Crossways Road, Grayshott

Annie and Isobel are out walking, dressed up, and in conversation

Annie What a glorious day, Izzy. Let's take a walk up to the turnpike and back.

Isobel And watch all those terrible women cycling past wearing their ghastly bloomers. What fun!

Annie Remember that one we saw last week, wearing a man's felt hat with a big long feather sticking up at the side?

Isobel Heavens yes! My mother would rather see me dead in my coffin than out dressed like that. Common, she calls it. Almost as bad as being one of those 'New Women'.

Annie The ones shouting 'Votes for Women!'

Isobel She says they're 'A lot of coarse great ugly things who can't get themselves husbands'.

Annie You should hear my father on about them. 'Give 'em votes?' he says, 'If I had my way I'd give 'em a good slap on the bottom and make 'em stay at home where they belong'.

Isobel I can't imagine people like that living here in the village though, can you Annie? Think of our friends—our little 'garden of girls'—there's none of them like that.

Annie There's a big, wide world outside Grayshott though, Izzy.

Isobel Now you're being clever. Remember our motto: 'Be good, sweet maid, and let who will be clever.'

Annie That's from Charles Kingsley.

Isobel And that's being clever again. Men don't like clever girls—you'll end up being an old maid if you're not careful, then you'll be sorry.

Annie *(Protesting)* I'm not being clever—I just enjoy reading, Izzy. Don't you? Don't you love Christina Rossetti for instance? She's my favourite.

'When I am dead my dearest, Sing no sad songs for me ... '

Isobel Oh, let's leave that dreary rot to the kids. Thank the gods and little fishes our schooldays are over!

Annie And we're out of the clutches of "Podgy" Ward.

Isobel And those dreadful inspections by Miss I'Anson. Do you remember her clipping Willie Harris round the ear that day?

Annie After saying it would hurt her more than it hurt him!

Isobel Throw the exercise books away! We're *fin de seekle* now.

Annie We're what?

Isobel *Fin de seekle.* It means 'end of the century'.

Annie Is that how you pronounce it?

Isobel I think so. Look, let's not start being clever again.

Annie Sorry. It's just that you make it sound like a bit of fish. I was imagining this poor 'seekle' swimming around in the local lakes.

Isobel Annie, stop being a tease! When were you last down by the lakes anyway? You've not been out walking with 'stalking Flora' have you?

Annie That's rotten of you, Izzy. She's a good friend of mine. We get on very well.

Isobel Always out on her own, talking to old men. I think that's weird, don't you?

Annie She knows a lot about the countryside.

Isobel Who wants to know about that? You can't marry the countryside can you? She should settle down and have a family. How old is she?

Annie Over twenty-one.

Isobel That's ancient!—and with no man in prospect yet.

Annie Well, I'm not going to be a gossip Izzy—I think it's *her* business, don't you?

Isobel No need to snap, dear Annie. I'm just glad that I have my Eric and you have your Arthur—at least we shan't get left on the shelf. Look, there's Martha and Fanny ahead—shall we catch them up and hear what gossip they've got?

Scene 7

In Grayshott Post Office, a few days later

Flora is busy serving young Winifred Storr and Grace ('Gee') Leuchars

Flora Right, Winifred, that's a half-crown postal order—and how many stamps?

Winifred How many cards did you buy, Gee?

Gee Just these two.

Winifred And I've got three.

Flora Five ha'penny stamps for the post-cards, then. That's tuppence ha'penny. Anything else?

Gee Should I get one for Madeleine?

Winifred That's up to you.

Gee What do you think?

Winifred She's coming back home tomorrow, Gee. You'll see her then,

Gee But if I send to the others and not to her …

Winifred Well get one if you think you should.

Gee She'll have left before it arrives though.

Winifred Not if it catches the next post. Ask Miss Timms.

Flora You've just missed one, I'm afraid.

Winifred I tell you what—buy her a card now and give it to her when she arrives.

Gee Winifred, that's silly!

Winifred It's the thought that counts, my granny says.

Gee No—it's not the same if it's not properly posted.

Winifred Well, are you or aren't you? Make up your mind.

Gee I can't decide.

Flora You only live just round the corner, Grace. You can always pop back if you change your mind.

Winifred Yes—and I've got to cycle all the way back to Hindhead. Come on.

Gee All right, I'll leave it for now.

Flora Right. That's two and sixpence plus a penny poundage for the postal order, and tuppence ha'penny for the stamps—two and ninepence ha'penny then, please. Who's paying?

Winifred I'll pay—the postal order's for granny. *(She hands Flora some coins)*

Flora So—you've given me three shillings—and there's tuppence ha'penny change. Is that right?

Winifred *(Calculating)* Er—yes.

Flora *(Laughing)* But only just, eh?

Gee *(To Winifred)* I owe you a penny.

Winifred Oh never mind that. Let's go and write these cards in your house now, then we can come back and put them in the box.

Flora Goodbye. Good writing.

Winifred & Gee *(As they exit)* Goodbye.

> *Emily Chapman has been in the shop for the last few moments.*
> *She comes over to Flora*

Emily Chapman Nice girls.

Flora Yes, charming.

Emily Chapman From good families.

Flora So I believe.

Emily Chapman *(Distantly)* Lucky children.

Flora *(Hesitantly)* Are you feeling all right, Mrs Chapman?

Emily Chapman Yes—yes, thank you. *(A pause)* I fear we embarrassed you the other night.

Flora The other night?

Emily Chapman When you brought the cash into the house at the end of business. My husband and I were … Well, it must have been embarrassing for you. I'm sorry.

Flora No, really …

Emily Chapman Me sitting there on the hearthrug with my head on my husband's knee—you must have wondered …

Flora It was nothing. In fact I was very glad to see you looking so happy.

Emily Chapman Happy. For once. Yes, I suppose I was. *(A pause)* It's not easy—a young girl like you living in, and with a family like ours.

Flora *(Carefully)* I am quite comfortable here.

Emily Chapman Are you? With the footsteps outside your bedroom in the middle of the night? Don't tell me you haven't heard them. I've seen the way you've looked at him sometimes the next morning.

Flora Mrs Chapman! You're surely not accusing me of …

Emily Chapman No, my dear. I'm accusing you of nothing other than being a respectable young girl in a difficult situation. My husband wasn't always like this, you know. Does he frighten you?

Flora Mr Chapman? He …

Emily Chapman He's a man of changing moods. He was very much in love with Letitia, you know—Letty as he calls her.

Flora I've heard him mention her.

Emily Chapman His childhood sweetheart—but her father wouldn't let them marry until Walter had proved himself, earning good money.

Flora And did he?

Emily Chapman Earn money? Yes, eventually, but only by emigrating to Australia for several years. Then, just when he'd booked his passage home with enough money to satisfy even her father, he received a wire: 'Return at once—Letty ill'.

Flora How terrible!

Emily Chapman And in the hurry and confusion of trying to get home quickly, he went down with heat-stroke—it's affected him ever since.

Flora And Letty?

Emily Chapman That's the real tragedy. She died two days before he docked at Southampton. Instead of a wedding, he arrived for a funeral. The shock was almost too much for him to bear. He vowed then never to marry as long as he lived.

Flora But he married you.

Emily Chapman Twenty years afterwards. I suppose he thought time had healed the pain sufficiently. *(A pause)* You know, he can be the most loving of men at times.

Flora I find him very civil.

Emily Chapman And in his trade as a cabinet maker he is second to none.

Flora So I believe.

Emily Chapman It's just that occasionally … I do wish he'd talk to the doctor about it. *(A pause)* But why am I bothering you with all my problems? You have your own life to live.

Flora Would it be easier for you if I looked for lodgings somewhere else?

Emily Chapman Where would you find anything you could afford? They ask two guineas a week for a front room here in the season—that's twice what you earn.

Flora I'm sure there must be somewhere.

Emily Chapman Don't worry—we'll manage all right with you here.

Two customers enter

I must get back to my children. I just wanted to apologise …

Flora It's all right, Mrs Chapman. Thank you.

The customers are Arthur Conan Doyle and George Bernard Shaw,
deep in conversation

Shaw To be sure, I've never seen anything so abysmal in my life. Never.

Doyle It received a great deal of praise in the local press.

Shaw It did, and that's what concerns me. They might be tempted to repeat the performance. That's why I'm sending off my own account of it to *The Herald*.

Doyle You didn't expect a professional London performance from our poor country amateurs, did you?

Shaw There is a difference, my dear Doyle, between an amateur performance and an amateurish presentation.

Doyle There is?

Shaw There is indeed. As far as the acting was concerned, I was not too unhappy. I have seen all the parts worse done at one time or another by professional actors at first-rate London theatres—though I confess that's not saying very much these days.

Doyle The Bard is not the easiest author to play.

Shaw But they removed all the difficult bits. It wasn't *As You Like It* that we saw there in Pollock's woods—it was a version with all the seriously unflattering characters cut out.

Doyle A sort of 'As You *Didn't* Like It'.

Shaw Those parts they left in virtually acted themselves, even with rank amateurs playing them. But what really made my heart sink was seeing the cottage piano on the set.

Doyle A piano, in Sir Frederick's woods?

Shaw I knew that people who would put a piano outside in the forest of Arden would do anything, and the event fulfilled my worst apprehensions. Why should Amiens sing to a banging drawing-room accompaniment? Why should Silvius struggle in vain in a tunic made for a much smaller man? Why will gentlemen who would rather die than walk down Bond Street in my hat, happily wear any second-hand misfit in a Shakespeare play?

Doyle Ha!

Shaw And why must everyone wear tights? It seems impossible to persuade an amateur that he is acting unless he has tights on.

Doyle Don't you think you're being a bit hard on a local event run to raise money for charity?

Shaw It doesn't bear remembering. I went to it in the most amiable disposition, and at the end no prudent person would have trusted me with a thunderbolt.

Doyle Well they won't invite you again.

Shaw That's the only consolation I have in it. *(To Flora)* A stamp if you please for this broadside.

Doyle You seem to be walking a little better now.

Shaw On my 'insidious injury,' as one reporter called it? Amazing what emotions a sprained ankle can cause in the press, isn't it. I've told them I'm now well on the road to recovery, and no more bulletins will be issued. *(To Flora, taking the stamp)* Thank you.

Doyle When do we next take the platform together? *(To Flora)* May I have two shillings worth of stamps, please?

Shaw I shall be talking to the local Band of Mercy again soon, about the evils of meat eating.

Doyle I don't think you'd want me along for that.

Shaw Does Holmes eat meat?

Doyle He generally has more urgent things to do. *(To Flora, taking the stamps)* Thank you very much. There has been no telegram arrived for Doyle?

Flora Doyle? No, sir. We would send it out to you as soon as one arrived.

Shaw And now he has cheated the Reichenbach Falls, what further great exploits may we expect of him?

Doyle Nothing more strenuous than pursuing a Solitary Cyclist down the Farnham Road at the moment.

Shaw And I'll wager he has the subservient Watson do that for him anyway.

They exit

Flora *(To herself)* How can I ever think of myself as a writer with people like Mr Conan Doyle around me?

Marion enters

Marion Did you see who that was, Flora?

Flora Mr Doyle and Mr Shaw.

Marion Mr Doyle—I wish <u>he</u> could help me with my speech.

Flora Well, you'll have to make do with me, Marion. How's it coming along?

Marion Not very well, I'm afraid. Look, I've tried to write something, but it isn't enough, is it? *(She shows Flora her notebook)*

Flora Your handwriting's awfully spread out. This speech wouldn't last more than a minute.

Marion That's what I mean.

Flora And I think you'll have to change that sentence there—it doesn't read very well as it stands.

Marion Oh dear—now you're making it even shorter.

Flora You'll just have to think of more things to say.

Marion But what else can I say? I've run out of ideas.

Flora Well look, I can't do anything about it now. Would you like me or Annie to come round to your house, to help you with it?

Marion Oh Flora, would you? I can't tell you how worried it's been making me.

Flora I can see. You're starting to droop at the edges. I'll talk to Annie about it tomorrow and see what we can do.

William Sillick enters

Marion Bless you. I'd be ever so grateful. Oh, and here's the fruit drops I promised you. *(Gives a bag to Flora)*

Flora Marion, thank you—you shouldn't have.

Marion That's all right—you can share them with Annie. Thank you again for what you've done. Goodbye for now. *(To Sillick)* Mr Sillick. *(She exits)*

Flora Goodbye Marion. *(To Sillick)* How to solve 'The Case of the Worried Speechwriter.' Elementary, my dear Flora!

Sillick What bribery and corruption is this?

Flora Nothing suitable for your newspaper, William.

Sillick But I saw a package change hands. Has the Christian Endeavour movement sunk to this?

Flora Front page in the *Herald* next week—'Scandal exposed on Hindhead'.

Sillick 'Your reporter's eye-witness account of a furtive dealing in fruit drops.'

Flora 'Church denies decay in morals,' or should that be molars?

Sillick Something like that. You're in the wrong job Flora.

Flora You think I could earn a living as a headline writer?

Sillick Perhaps—but not here. There's only one living to be earned as a reporter in this village.

Flora And that position's already taken.

Sillick So long as I keep bringing them in the news, all the news and nothing but the news.

Flora Which is why you've come in to see me.

Sillick I did catch a glimpse of two eminent gentlemen leaving your door just now.

Flora And you're hoping I might divulge some trade secrets—but you know me better than that.

Sillick I do. And so I've a better plan.

Flora Tell me, good sir, what do you have in mind?

Sillick A good long tramp across the moors next Sunday, with stewed whortleberries and cream tea at the *Seven Thorns* afterwards. How about that?

Flora I'd enjoy that very much.

Sillick Then I'll be here for you at ten when you close … *(Looking out of the window)* Ah, there goes Mr Doyle now—must see if I can catch him. *(Making for the door)* Sunday then.

Flora *(After him)* Sunday, William—thank you. *(Lights fade on her)*

Sillick *(Chasing up the road)* Mr Doyle—have you a moment, sir? A word with you if I may—for the *Herald* …

Scene 8

Inside the Chapmans' accommodation at Grayshott Post Office, that night

Walter and Emily Chapman are arguing off-stage

Emily Chapman Walter, what's the matter now? Come back to bed.

Walter Chapman They're here again! They're after me! Can't you hear them?

Emily Chapman Nobody's after you.

Walter Chapman They're here I tell you! Whispering under the window. Outside.

Emily Chapman It's the middle of the night, Walter. Calm down. You'll wake everybody up.

Walter Chapman I don't care about everybody. It's not everybody they're after—it's me they're after!

They both emerge onto the stage in night-clothes.
Walter has a revolver in his hand

Emily Chapman Come back to bed—and please give me that gun.

Walter Chapman Burglars!

Emily Chapman There's no-one.

Walter Chapman   You'll not get me, whoever you are!   *(He points the revolver through a window and fires)*   Take that!

Emily Chapman   *(Screaming)*   Walter, no!

Walter Chapman   There's more where that came from!

Emily Chapman   Give me the gun, for God's sake!

Walter Chapman   More where that came from.

Flora rushes on, also in night-clothes

Flora   What's happening?

Emily Chapman   It's all right, Flora.   Go back to bed.

Walter Chapman   *(To no-one in particular)*   You'll not get me.

Flora   What was that bang?

Emily Chapman   Nothing.   Mr Chapman is just having a bad night, that's all.

Walter Chapman   *(Hissing)*   Revenge is mine!

Emily Chapman   Go back to bed, Flora—we'll be all right.   We'll be all right.

Emily leads Walter off—Flora stands a while, watching their exit

Flora   A bad night?   He had a gun in his hand, and I've no lock on my door!   The man's insane.   He could murder us all at any time.   I can't stay here any longer.

Emily reappears

Emily Chapman   Go to bed, Flora—it's all right now.

Flora tries to speak, but then turns silently and exits

Please God, let it be all right now!   *(Emily exits again)*

Scene 9

In Grayshott Post Office, a few days later

Annie is serving Mr Foreshaw

Annie   A five shilling postal order, Mr Foreshaw—there you are—that will be five shillings and a penny, please.

Foreshaw   *(Paying)*   And where is our postmistress today?

Annie   Miss Timms?   She'll be back shortly.   She's just popped out to see her new landlady.

Foreshaw   I see.

Annie   Did you want her for anything?

Foreshaw No, no. She was good enough to deliver a telegram to me the other evening, after hours. Very kind. Very helpful.

Annie What, after we'd closed?

Foreshaw Old colleague from Africa—Zambesi valley '84—just about to board a train at Waterloo—sent me a wire from there to say he was on his way. First I knew of it.

Annie And Flora brought it round to you herself?

Foreshaw Sat her down and gave her a glass of fruit juice for her trouble. She seemed fascinated by all my maps.

Annie I see.

Foreshaw Just wondering if she might come round again. Well, I'll not keep you from your work. Good day.

Annie Goodbye, Mr Foreshaw—I'll tell her you called.

As Foreshaw exits, Walter Chapman enters from the house
holding a sheaf of papers

Walter Chapman Is Miss Timms not here?

Annie No, Mr Chapman—she's just …

Walter Chapman No matter. There's some correspondence here from London which she must look at. Complaint from Headquarters about late delivery of a telegram.

Annie Late delivery?

Walter Chapman That's what I said. Miss Timms has responsibility for this office, so she must answer it. I have my cabinet-making to attend to.

Annie Yes, Mr Chapman.

Walter Chapman *(He is about to exit, then turns)* I gather she has found herself new lodgings.

Annie *(Hesitantly)* Yes—with Mrs Parkhurst. Just down the road.

Walter Chapman *(Musingly)* Just down the road. She's happy there?

Annie I believe so.

Walter Chapman Good—good. *(Back to business)* Make sure she sees the papers, will you? *(He exits)*

Annie *(To herself)* There's enough of them!

Flora enters from the street

Flora Well that's done—rent paid in advance.

Annie Oh good. Mr Chapman was just asking how you liked your new place.

Flora What did you say?

Annie I said I thought you did.

Flora I do. My own room with my own fire. I can shut the door on the world—it'll be a haven of peace.

Annie I'd go 'barmy on the crumpet' sitting up there all by myself of an evening, with no-one to talk to.

Flora I'll read, and do a bit of writing. It's what I enjoy.

Annie Well, rather you than me. Oh, your old man was in here just now too, asking after you.

Flora Mr Foreshaw?

Annie He said you'd been round to see him.

Flora Yes, I did. To …

Annie & Flora (Together) … deliver a telegram.

Annie Yes. At night. And now he's asking if you'd like to go round again.

Flora Oh, come on, Annie. It's not like that—he seems a very nice old gentleman. And so many stories of Africa to tell. He was a big-game hunter once, you know.

Annie I can't understand you, Flora, really I can't. You're either sitting on your own in a little bare room, or you're out talking with strange old men. If you want to go out, why not come round to tea at my house—and afterwards we'll take a stroll up the road with my Arthur.

Flora That's very kind of you, Annie, but I'm not sure Arthur would really want me along playing 'gooseberry.'

Annie *(A little hurt)* Well, now you're back I must be off home for dinner. *(She puts her hat on)*

Flora What's this pile of papers?

Annie Oh, sorry, I forgot. Mr Chapman brought them out. A complaint from Head Office, he says. *(She puts her coat on)*

Flora *(Flicks through the papers)* All this to do with the late delivery of a telegram?

Annie Seems a bit unfair when you go to the trouble of making personal deliveries out of hours, doesn't it.

Flora It was the time we had that terrific thunder-storm, remember?

Annie When old Marshall's cow was struck dead in the field just at the back here.

Flora And young Alfred came in soaked to the skin from making the last delivery. *[Alfred enters from outside at this moment]* Well, talk of the

Devil, here he is. We were just talking about that thunder storm last week.

Alf A monsoon, my dad called it!

Flora According to this, we were supposed to send you straight back out again.

Alf Nearly drowned, I was—down at Pook's Hill.

Flora Mrs Lyndon complained because we took an hour to deliver her message.

Alf Oh, <u>she</u> would.

Annie But we asked Mr Chapman at the time—he said we couldn't possibly.

Flora I know, but now *I* have to answer. It says, *'Climatic conditions are no excuse for the non-delivery of a telegram when a messenger is available. You will return these papers with the telegram properly endorsed and an undertaking that no similar incident occurs in future.'*

(Alf exits to inside room during this)

Annie *(Laughing)* Flora, how are we supposed to control the weather?

Flora I don't know, but 'Head Office expects' so we'll just have to try. I'll write something suitably apologetic and hope we hear no more.

Marion bursts in from outside

Marion Annie! Flora! I did it! I still can't believe it's true.

Annie Oh, your talk. It was last night wasn't it. How did it go?

Marion Wonderfully! The script that you and Flora wrote for me—and with me wearing my new frock—and taking the cab to the door …

Flora A cab to the door? But it's only a short walk from your house.

Marion Proper speakers always arrive in cabs Flora—it makes the occasion.

Annie Well, if you say so Marion. Anyway, I'm glad it was such a success.

Marion Oh it was. Thank you so much for your help—and Flora. I don't know what I'd have done.

Flora *(To Annie)* You'd better go for your dinner.

Annie Right. I'll be back in an hour—weather permitting! Come along, Marion—you can tell me all about it as we go. *(They exit to the street)*

Flora Well, I'd better start to earn my keep as a creative writer I suppose. *(Writing)* 'Error regretted. Care shall be taken that it does not occur again.' There! Fairly meaningless, but it should keep them happy.

Scene 10

In Crossways Road, Grayshott, soon after

*Ernest Chapman appears, bearded & wearing a 'Boer' hat,
and meets his brother Walter*

Walter Chapman You shame us, Ernest, by wearing that hat.

Ernest Chapman Shame, brother? It's this nation that should be dying of shame. Killing off good, honest, hard-working farmers and putting their women and children in concentration camps—just because they get in the way of our Imperialist plans for expansion.

Walter Chapman You'd let Kruger and his crew get away with all the insults and violence they've shown to our people out there?

Ernest Chapman You know nothing about it, Walter. Only what you read in the newspapers, and they're not going to report both sides of the argument equally.

Walter Chapman What makes you think you know better?

Ernest Chapman Common sense and a trust in the Lord. The Boers are a god-fearing people.

Walter Chapman Aye, so I'm told—a Bible in one hand and a brandy bottle in the other!

Ernest Chapman It doesn't take much Government propaganda to pull the wool over your eyes.

Walter Chapman Nobody's pulling the wool over anybody's eyes, Ernest. The whole of the village, except you, is in favour of this war.

Ernest Chapman That doesn't make them right.

Walter Chapman You should hear Mr Conan Doyle speak on the subject— that would change your mind.

Ernest Chapman I did, the other night, and it changed my mind not one jot. Fame does not ensure veracity, Walter. He can be as wrong as any other man.

Walter Chapman Well there's many folk around here with men going to the front, including my young assistant, and they don't want to see you going about sporting for the enemy.

Ernest Chapman Miss Timms? I wasn't aware she had a young man.

Walter Chapman Her brother. He was on the point of emigrating to Canada, she tells us, but now he's volunteered for the war instead.

Ernest Chapman I wish I could welcome such patriotism—but I fear it's misplaced.

Walter Chapman I'm no jingoist, brother, as well you know, but your attitude is insulting to the ordinary people here—and it's also bad for business.

Ernest Chapman Ha! I wondered when we'd get round to that. Well, for better or worse, if people in the village want their pipes unfrozen or their roof-tiles fixed, they've no choice but to come to me for it. If they don't want to speak to me the rest of the time, it's no great hardship.

Walter Chapman They have their principles.

Ernest Chapman <u>They</u> have principles? Well I'd hate to be around when they've lost them. I have my faith in the Lord to guide me, Walter, and that's enough for me.

Walter Chapman The Church of England begs to differ.

Ernest Chapman The established church is out of touch and out of date. I may not agree with everything that Mr Bernard Shaw says but, in that at least, I am on his side.

Walter Chapman Ironic, then, that his new Refreshment House is to be opened by a bishop's wife.

Ernest Chapman There are many ironies in life, brother. We must agree to differ as usual, but here—my hand—no hard feelings?

Walter Chapman None that can't be reconciled by healthy argument. I'll agree with that at least.

Scene 11

In Mr Foreshaw's House, next Sunday afternoon

He and Flora are looking at artefacts and maps hanging on the wall

Foreshaw That elephant's tusk there? There's a story behind that too.

Flora You seem to have a story for everything.

Foreshaw What's the point in keeping something if there's no story? This feller was nearly the end of me.

Flora How was that?

Foreshaw The platform I was standing on suddenly gave way—there I was lying sprawled on the ground in front of him. My boys all disappeared like streaks of greased lightning—left me alone, right in his path. I'd wounded him and he was charging straight at me.

Flora What happened?

Foreshaw He collapsed and died just before he got to me. Now what d'you think of these?

Flora Butterflies—but such glorious colours—they look almost painted.

Foreshaw Pretty things—you like them, eh?

Flora I should prefer to see them alive.

Foreshaw For that you would have to travel to East Africa.

Flora How long were you there?

Foreshaw Thirty years, near enough. Hunting and prospecting.

Flora You must find it awfully dull, living round here now.

Foreshaw Dull? Yes, damned dull. I feel old and cold and as dull as ditch-water. Shan't be sorry to go.

Flora Go where?

Foreshaw Wherever old hunters do go. Did I ever tell you I once found an elephants' cemetery? In a swamp. Ivory by the ton! My boys were digging at it for a fortnight. Had to make a special shipment from Beira.

Flora You have no family?

Foreshaw Never married. Didn't want to leave some poor woman crying her eyes out every time I disappeared into the blue. Bad for the nerve. 'He rides swiftest who rides alone,' as that young feller Kipling puts it. D'you read Kipling?

Flora I read anything and everything.

Foreshaw Good, good. Can't abide most of these new men myself, though. Give me Dickens or Thackeray any day. Always carried them with me on expeditions. Look—see this copy of *Great Expectations*—see the holes in it? Know what made those?

Flora They look like small shot-holes.

Foreshaw White ants—termites. Bore through anything they will. Not boring *you*, am I?

Flora Far from it—I could stay listening to your stories for ever.

Foreshaw Well, you're more than welcome. Only other visitor I get here is the doctor—comes to play chess and check my heart.

Flora I was warned you might be a bit of a woman-hater.

Foreshaw *(Laughing)* Not a hater of women between the ages of fifteen and fifty. But old women of either sex, I absolutely abominate them. Here, it's time for a cup of tea—and I've got some guava jelly in the larder, I'll wager you've never tasted that before.

Flora Not that I can remember.

Foreshaw There's a little room if you want to curl your hair or anything while I'm brewing. I'm an old bachelor, so I may have forgotten some of the things you ladies need—but I've put you out a bottle of eau-de-cologne.

Flora I feel like Mrs Micawber when she went to supper with David!

Foreshaw And after tea we can look at some of my books on Africa—I buy every new one published, you know. You can stay for a while longer?

Flora Sunday afternoons are free time for me.

Foreshaw Good. It's a change to find somebody who's interested. It would be nice to think someone like you could look after my things here when I'm gone. They'll just be scattered and knocked about by strangers otherwise.

Flora I'm sure there's many years in you yet.

Foreshaw Not so sure myself. I've cheated death too many times—snake bites, drought, wild animals, hostile natives … Takes it out of a body in the end. But enough of this maudlin talk—get yourself spruced up, and I'll make the tea.

Scene 12

In Crossways Road, Grayshott, a Sunday afternoon some weeks later

Isobel is waiting as Annie enters

Isobel There you are, Annie. I was beginning to think you were never coming.

Annie Sorry, Izzy. Mother wanted a 'talk' with me.

Isobel I thought I might have to take a walk on my own.

Annie *(Teasing)* That would never do! Well, I'm here—where shall we go?

Isobel Up to Fiveways and back?

Annie It's as good as anywhere. We can see how the Refreshment House is coming along.

Isobel My father thinks it's an evil place. You should hear him. 'Just encourage the riff-raff into the village.'

Annie My father's against it for the opposite reason. He likes his pint, and thinks they won't serve him there.

Isobel I wonder who *will* use it then.

Annie We'll find out when it opens, I suppose. Next week isn't it?

Isobel Well, I know *I* won't be there. What did your mother want to talk about?

Annie The usual—when is Arthur going to name the day.

Isobel Well, when *is* he going to name the day?

Annie Oh Izzy, *I* don't know. Don't let's talk about it.

Isobel This isn't my usual bubbly Annie.

Annie No it isn't. Sometimes I wish we girls could be left to sort our own lives out.

Isobel And a proper mess we'd make of it. Parents do know best, you know.

Annie Look at Flora though—independent, does what she wants and enjoys it. No parents around to tell her what to do and what not to do …

Isobel Well *she's* hardly an example to look up to. Goodness knows, the stories going round about her—you must have heard them.

Annie By people who don't know her.

Isobel I suppose she's round having tea with her old big-game hunter as usual.

Annie No, actually she's taken the train to Aldershot today, to see her brother—he's being drafted to South Africa.

Isobel *(Wind taken out of her sails a bit)* Oh.

Annie He's only nineteen. She's very worried about him, but she won't let it show. 'Never flinch,' she keeps saying.

Isobel And now she's living down with that Mrs Parkhurst. All those children crawling over the house, and no carpet on the stairs I'm told. What a life!

Annie Izzy, you're a snob!

Isobel My mother isn't rich, Annie, but at least she keeps the house clean and tidy.

Annie You're not poor. Your father runs his own business …

Isobel He has to work jolly hard at it.

Annie And there are only three of you to look after.

Isobel Annie—you can go off people, you know.

Annie Sorry. Are we still friends?

Isobel Still friends.

Annie Then *(acting tipsy)* let's go to the pub!

Isobel *(Laughing)* Very *fin de seekle*!

                    They start to walk off arm in arm

Annie Have you heard what they're going to call it?

Isobel No, what?

Annie The *Fox and Pelican*.

Isobel The what?

Annie The *Fox and Pelican*. Apparently Sir Frederick Pollock chose the name.

Isobel I wonder why?

Annie I could tell you, Izzy, but I won't, because you'd only say I was being clever again!

Scene 13

The opening of the Fox & Pelican, Grayshott

Sir Frederick Pollock introduces Mrs Davidson,
wife of the Bishop of Winchester

Pollock Ladies and gentlemen—as Chairman of the Association, it gives me great pleasure to introduce Mrs Randall Davidson, wife of the Bishop of Winchester, to open our Refreshment House here today. Dr Davidson himself was unable to come, but sends us his best wishes and his full-hearted support for the enterprise.

Given the great interest of the diocese in this project, I believe the name we have chosen for it is particularly fitting, deriving as it does from that great humanist Richard Fox—a previous Bishop of Winchester in the reign of Henry VIII—and the symbol of his notable foundation, Corpus Christi College, which is the Pelican.

So many people have been involved in the scheme that it would be unfair of me to attempt a list of benefactors. Sufficient to say that the £2,000 required for building and furnishings was forthcoming in a very short period of time. In addition we have to thank a number of people for gifts in kind: including Mr Bernard Shaw, who has given us a small but formidable library of books; and Walter Crane, principal of the Royal College of Art, who has painted us a mighty pretty signboard. It is perhaps the only such signboard in the land to have received an Episcopal blessing!

And with that in mind, let me now call upon Mrs Davidson to perform the opening ceremony.

There is general applause

Mrs Davidson Thank you, Sir Frederick, for that kind introduction. I must say it is not every day that I am invited to open a public house. Indeed, I am aware that some people may find my involvement in such an enterprise distasteful—not their cup of tea, if you will excuse the pun. To them I apologise, but if I did not believe these schemes to be in the best interests of temperance generally, I assure you I should not be here ....

The light fades on her as she continues, and comes up on William Sillick
and a local man in the bar

Sillick Good day, sir—for the *Herald*. May I ask, are you a resident of this village?

Man I am that.

Sillick And how do you like your new pub?

Man It's all right.

Sillick No more than 'all right'?

Man Sight too much green paint around, if you ask me. Apart from that …

Sillick I see you're drinking the beer though.

Man Aye, the mild's not bad. Tuppence-ha'penny a pint. Thruppence for bitter and stout.

Sillick You're not tempted to try the ginger beer or lemonade, then.

Man Are you? Stick to beer, says I. Not a bad brew this either. Want to try some.

Sillick I'm not a great beer drinker myself.

Man Oh ar. Spirits man are you? The landlord's come from the Navy, I'm told—p'raps he'll get you a tot of rum if you ask.

Sillick He sells spirits?

Man He does too, but they're hidden away—same as the beer is. There's always the coffee of course.

Sillick Is there indeed?—I think perhaps I might give that a try. Keep a clear head.

Man Through the door over there, then. They say that's the coffee room.

The light fades, and comes up on Mrs Davidson again

Mrs Davidson … and whether your want is a coffee or whether your taste is to something a little stronger, I am sure that the excellent Association which has worked so hard to promote this project within the village will make of it a great success in the future. And so now, without further ado, I declare this Refreshment House—the *Fox and Pelican*—open.

There is general applause, and the lights fade

Scene 14

In Grayshott Post Office, a few days later

Flora is behind the counter—Annie enters with two large covered plates

Annie Here you are Flora—hope you're hungry! Compliments of the *Fox & Pelican*.

Flora I thought you were going home to eat.

Annie I am. These are both for you. Dinner, and pudding.

Flora Let me have a look. *(She looks under the lids)* Annie, they're immense!

Annie It's a good ninepenny-worth.

Flora Look at that roly-poly! There's enough for three of my appetite here.

Annie Perhaps Mrs Chapman will keep some back and heat it up for you again tomorrow.

Flora I could ask her.

Annie I saw Martha and Fanny just now. Can you believe it?—they're wearing khaki!

Flora It's the new fashionable colour. People are starting to realise there's a war on.

Annie And their sailor hats—they've put red, white and blue stripes round them.

Flora Very patriotic.

Annie They said they were going to walk up and down outside Mr Chapman's brother's house—just to show what they think of him and his Boer hat.

Flora *(In jest)* They'd better be careful—they'll be 'New Women' before they know it. Demonstrating on the streets—whatever next!

Annie And your brother's out there now, Flora. I'm sorry—I forgot.

Flora Edwin can look after himself—he'll not flinch. *(Pause)* Thanks for bringing the dinner.

Annie That's all right. I'll be off home—see you later.

Annie exits again to the street. Flora takes the lid off a plate

Flora *(To herself)* Enough here to feed an army! I do hope you'll be all right out there, Edwin.

Walter Chapman enters from the house with papers in his hand

Walter Chapman Miss Timms, another directive from Head Office, I'm afraid.

Flora Not about that late delivery again.

Walter Chapman No, no—they seem to have forgotten about that now. It's the war in South Africa.

Flora Ah, yes.

Walter Chapman In future, telegraph offices are to post a bulletin in the window every Sunday morning, to let the general public know how things are going.

Flora When shall we receive it?

Walter Chapman By ten o'clock in the morning—normal Sunday closing time, it says here—but they expect you to wait for it if it's late.

Flora On a Sunday. For how long?

Walter Chapman That they don't say. They obviously rely on your sense of duty, to remain at your post at a time of National crisis.

Flora Yes, of course.

Walter Chapman I assume you'll have no difficulty in staying if necessary. You have no family to worry about.

Flora Not here in the village.

Walter Chapman No. And I'm certain the good Mrs Parkhurst will keep your dinner hot for you if necessary.

Flora *(Looking at her own dinner getting cold)* Yes, I'm sure she would.

Walter Chapman Then let us consider the matter dealt with. *(Hands her the papers)*

Flora *(Without too much irony)* Thank you, Mr Chapman.

Walter Chapman Now I must go across the road and ask my brother to fix a loose roof tile for me. That's assuming he's still trading with supporters of the Government!

Chapman exits to the street

Flora *(To herself)* Goodbye Sunday morning walks! Never mind—I'm still young, with plenty of walking years ahead of me. *(Starts picking at her food)* Mr Foreshaw knows Africa—perhaps he can tell me about all the names mentioned in the bulletins. And about the places where Edwin will be ... Tell me he's nothing to fear from poor Boer farmers, compared with charging elephants and poisonous snakes. My dear old gentleman! Will you ever marry and lead a 'normal' life, Flora? The sort of life everyone expects you to lead. No more bumping into Bob Pikesley on the common —no more illicit afternoons taking tea with Mr Foreshaw—no more freedom ... But what freedom have *you* got at the moment, Edwin? It was going to be a new life in Canada for you, but now ... *(Close to tears—but then she controls it)* Flora, you didn't flinch did you? You didn't flinch! What was it mother used to say? 'We are as we are made.' Eat your ninepenny lunch, my girl, and let the world worry about itself for a change.

Music: Boer War tunes during interval

— INTERVAL —

Scene 15

In Grayshott Post Office, 1901

Flora and Annie behind the counter, still in light mourning for the Queen - Music: 'Soldiers of the Queen' by a brass band comes from outside

Annie You're looking positively radiant today, Flora—what's the secret?

Flora Annie! I'm sure I'm no different from yesterday.

Annie Perhaps. I don't know though. I think it's that Richard Brownlow—he's been in here a lot recently, hasn't he?

Flora Nonsense. You're always trying to pair me off with somebody. Richard and I are …

Together … just good friends.

Annie *(Laughing)* Exactly!

Flora He's been down here from London with his sister, visiting relatives.

Annie Several times.

Flora I get on just as well with Mavis.

Annie Lucky she is only his sister though. If she was anything else, you'd be jealous.

Flora I would not.

Annie No? 'The lady doth protest too much, methinks.'

Flora 'Oh, but she'll keep her word.'

Together Hamlet!

Annie But *what* word will she keep?

Flora Ah, that's for the play to expose. This 'she' keeps her own counsel.

Annie *(Agreeing)* She does. You're as deep as the day I met you, over two years ago.

Flora *(Listening to the band)* They're still playing out there.

Annie I suppose it's 'Soldiers of the King' now. There's not too many people around who can still remember a king, are there?

Flora You'd have to be in your seventies.

Annie 'Granny' Robinson next door remembers the first train coming to Haslemere. But she was only one when the last king died. *(Pause)* What are they playing for?

Flora Funds for the war effort, I imagine.

43

Annie I thought the war was nearly over.

Flora My brother's still out there.

Annie Can't be long now though, can it?

Flora Let's hope not. Perhaps I should try to finish this scarf before it all ends—what d'you think? And send it over to Edwin to keep him warm.

She gets out a long, wide scarf of scarlet wool, on woollen needles

Annie *(Laughing)* Oh Flora, it's ridiculous—that colour.

Flora I was given this wool by the relief organisation—not my choice. Keep the boys warm, they said.

Annie It'd make a good mark for one of the Boer snipers to fire at.

Flora That's what everyone says. Perhaps I'd just as well not finish it.

Annie At least you <u>can</u> knit. It's almost a lost art round here. I can't.

Flora That's because you didn't grow up in a homely little village with no shops. We had to make most everything ourselves.

Annie 'Most everything'—makes you sound like a real country yokel.

Flora *(Playing up to her)* Lawk 'a' mussy-O, missy — where be 'ee a-gooin'?

Annie Lucky you don't talk like that to the customers!

Flora I used to speak like it to Mr Foreshaw. It made him laugh.

Annie You miss him, don't you—your old man.

Flora Very much. For weeks afterwards I kept thinking, "Oh, I must remember to tell Mr Foreshaw that"—then I suddenly realised I couldn't any more. *(Pause)* You know, I went down on the Sunday after they buried him—just to see where the old hunter had ended up.

Annie Did you approve?

Flora It's a nice little churchyard there in the mother village. I like to think he's at peace now—close to the old, mellow stone church tower—very English.

Annie That's nice.

Flora I bought a him bunch of red roses from the shop by the church gate, and left them on his grave. There were two other wreaths from the funeral there—wax ones, from his sister and a nephew. D'you know, he'd never mentioned his family to me.

Annie Sounds as though he was as close with his thoughts as you are.

Flora Yes, perhaps we were two of a kind in a peculiar sort of way. Anyway, I walked back in the sunshine over the heath—that cheered me up a bit. Purple as far as the eye could see—and the birches and the green bracken—and the air filled with the scent of heather and pine …

Richard Brownlow enters from the street

Richard Hello, I see Flora's expounding on the splendours of the local countryside again.

Annie Richard, you've just broken the spell.

Richard What spell?

Annie Flora was getting all maudlin about Mr Foreshaw.

Richard I'd like to have met him—he seemed quite a character.

Flora He was. You should have seen inside his bungalow.

Annie They auctioned off his belongings shortly after he died. I remember people coming past the post office carrying all sorts of weird things—one boy with antlers on his head!

Flora I'd have loved to have gone along and picked up a memento or two, but I couldn't get away.

Richard You've got nothing of his?

Flora He always said he'd like to leave me something, a book perhaps—but never mind … *(Mock serious)* Now what can I do for you, sir? Postage stamps? Postal Orders?

Richard You can put your knitting down, and take Mavis and me off and away into this earthly paradise you describe so well.

Flora Is it closing time already?

Richard Near enough.

Annie She was miles away.

Flora I'll just have to cash up. Can you wait?

Annie We've had a very busy day up until half an hour ago. We were just relaxing.

Richard How will the new telegraph office up the road affect you?

Annie I don't know—take some trade away I suppose. But it's not due to open till later in the year.

Richard *(To Flora)* I'll be over the road in the *Fox & Pelican*—having a coffee with Mavis.

Annie Nothing stronger I hope.

Richard Well, maybe a small nip of brandy in it.

Flora Richard Brownlow, if we have to carry you home …

Richard I'll buy you one too, then you won't notice!

Flora Show him the door, Annie! *(To Richard)* I'll be over shortly.

Richard *(On his way out)* Where are you taking us today?

Flora To a place called Gibbet Hill, where they used to string up local murderers—and if you don't behave yourself, I'll string you up too!

Scene 16

In the Chapmans' accommodation at Grayshott Post Office

Walter and Emily are having a terrible row

Walter Chapman You're nothing but a common whore, woman. A strumpet.

Emily Chapman No, Walter!

Walter Chapman Years ago you'd be taken out and stoned.

Emily Chapman Walter, the children!

Walter Chapman They knew how to deal with harlots in those days. You bring shame to this house, woman.

Emily Chapman The children will be listening.

Walter Chapman Damn the children, and damn you!

Emily Chapman Walter, I've been faithful to you.

Walter Chapman Faithful? You're here in Letty's place—how can you be faithful? Tricked into marrying you, I was. Tricked then and tricked now!

Emily Chapman Walter ...

Walter Chapman Don't you Walter me—you cheap slut—I'll teach you ...

He is about to strike her when his brother Ernest enters and holds him

Ernest Chapman Brother, stop! For God's sake.

Emily Chapman Ernest, he's mad—he's trying to kill me!

Walter Chapman Kill? Not I. The Lord will repay. He will judge. Only He.

Ernest Chapman Quite so, brother, quite so. You must calm yourself or it will lead to something tragic.

Walter Chapman She has been unfaithful to me.

Emily Chapman When!—won't you tell me when?

Ernest Chapman I believe you are mistaken, Walter. I believe you are suffering under a delusion.

Walter Chapman So—even you would label me mad.

Ernest Chapman You have no right to treat your wife in this way.

Walter Chapman Even you would bind me and put me away.

Ernest Chapman Nobody's binding you, Walter, or putting you away. But you have no right to revenge yourself on your wife, even if what you say is true. As you have said, 'The Lord will judge—the Lord will repay'.

Walter Chapman *(To Emily)* It is only that text which has saved you from having a bullet through you.

Ernest Chapman Walter! Brother. Come with me and let this sorry woman alone. Maybe it would be best if you separate for a while—for a few weeks perhaps. Otherwise I fear the worst.

Walter Chapman They separated me from Letty! Made us live half a world apart. Parted us for ever.

Ernest Chapman Come.

Walter Chapman *(Hissing)* 'To be, or not to be … '

Ernest Chapman Walter—this way—with me.

> *He leads Walter off, motioning for Emily to stay behind.*
> *She sinks in a chair, sobbing*

Emily Chapman Letty's real to him, I'm not. How can I fight against a ghost? How can I?

Child's Voice *(from offstage)* Mumma! *(Louder)* Mumma!

Emily Chapman *(Wiping her eyes)* Yes, Lulu—what is it?

Child's Voice Are you all right, mumma?

Emily Chapman *(Rising)* Yes, dear, mumma's all right. Don't cry—mumma's all right. Back to bed now. Back to bed. Everything's all right—till the morning. *(She exits towards the voice)*

Scene 17

At Flora's lodgings with Mrs Parkhurst

Mrs Parkhurst is giving Flora a 'talking to'

Mrs Parkhurst Now then, young lady, what time of night do you call this? A quarter past eleven.

Flora I'm very sorry, Mrs Parkhurst.

Mrs Parkhurst And arriving unchaperoned with a young man I've never seen before. Richard, did you call him?

Flora He very kindly offered to walk with me …

Mrs Parkhurst From the public house?

Flora No, it was …

Mrs Parkhurst There was one of those dance things there tonight, wasn't there?

Flora I believe so, but I went to a lecture at the Congregational Hall.

Mrs Parkhurst *(A little deflated)* Oh. There'd be no dancing there.

Flora No, it was a London author talking about his novels. Very good.

Mrs Parkhurst He finished later than expected then?

Flora The audience kept asking questions—they wouldn't let him get away.

Mrs Parkhurst I've had to sit up waiting for you. Eleven o'clock we agreed. Mr Parkhurst went to bed—he has to get up for work in the morning.

Flora I'm sorry. It won't happen again.

Mrs Parkhurst Let's say no more then. You're a good girl and you help me around the house as best you can. Better than the men lodgers I've had before, any rate.

Flora Thank you.

Mrs Parkhurst The usual for breakfast at the usual time then. I'll say good night.

Flora Good night, Mrs Parkhurst.

Mrs Parkhurst *(As she exits)* And don't forget to put the guard in front of the fire.

Flora No, I won't Mrs Parkhurst.

Scene 18

Sir Frederick Pollock meets with Conan Doyle

Walking along the Portsmouth turnpike at Hindhead

Pollock Ah, Doyle—good morning. Out taking the air I see?

Doyle Making a virtue of necessity, Sir Frederick. I have to go down to the village to send off some wires.

Pollock Dashed inconvenient, eh? Sooner they open the telegraph office at Hindhead the better—especially for you—be just across the road from your back gate.

Doyle I really don't mind the walk in this sort of weather.

Pollock Trouble with our 'green and pleasant land'—this sort of weather's all too rare. Roads become a mudbath—and it seems an impertinence to take the horse out for such a short ride.

Doyle You could try a bicycle.

Pollock At my age? I think not.

Doyle Or invest in an automobile. They seem to be almost reliable these days.

Pollock Trouble with this area, Doyle, is that it's becoming too accessible, and the automobile will make it more so. Take your life in your hands crossing the Portsmouth road now. Mad fools driving them, got no common sense or courtesy for others.

Doyle I have a mind possibly to buy one myself next year.

Pollock Huh!

Doyle Which I hope to drive with both common sense and courtesy.

Pollock Well, no offence, but I'm beginning to think of moving somewhere more peaceful. Poor old Tyndall's to blame. Made such a song and dance about how healthy it was to live here that everybody wanted to come.

Doyle England's 'little Switzerland.'

Pollock That's what the guide books say. More's the pity.

Doyle Well, I must continue on my way—to assail our efficient young Grayshott postmistress with yet more work.

Pollock I wonder what she'll do when Hindhead opens?

Doyle Considerably less, I should think.

They part, with appropriate farewells, in separate directions

Scene 19

In Grayshott Post Office, soon after

Flora is about to take a half day off

Annie Seems strange here without Mrs Chapman around.

Flora Bit more than 'just a lovers' tiff' this time, it seems. They're saying in the village she's gone for good, with the children.

Annie I heard that she wanted to come back, but Mr Chapman wouldn't let her.

Flora Which Mr Chapman?

Annie Our Mr Chapman—her husband.

Flora That sounds sensible to me.

Annie Sensible? A man not wanting his wife and children back?

Flora I used to live here remember. I've seen things you haven't.

Annie What sort of things?

Flora I can't tell you that—I promised Mrs Chapman I wouldn't.

Annie You've got me all curious now.

Flora Well you'll have to stay curious! It's my half day, and I'm off to take Mavis and Richard for a walk over Ludshott Common.

Flora starts to put her hat and coat on

Annie Rather you than me. My Arthur would run a mile at the thought—'walking in the wilderness,' he'd call it.

Flora But Mavis and Richard are from London. They need to clean their lungs of all that city smoke. Your Arthur doesn't have to.

Annie Nor do you.

Flora No—but I enjoy it for it's own sake. I'll see you tomorrow.

Annie Tomorrow never comes.

Flora makes a 'face' at her and goes out to the street

Enjoy your walk. *(Pause)* I wonder what it is she can't tell me? Oh well, let's get these letters sorted while it's quiet. Pim-li-co—Nor-wich—Ye-o-vil—Willes-den—Slough, like a snake *(Willie enters from outside)* Ugh, no peace for the wicked.

Willie It's a long way to Mr Whitaker's.

Annie Grayshott Hall? It's only a mile and a half—and all on the flat.

Willie Seems a lot further.

Annie Well, you can have a rest now—nothing else to go out for the moment. And I can get on with this sorting.

Willie Not for long. That man who sends long ones is on his way—I saw him coming.

Annie The man who sends long ones?

Conan Doyle enters

Willie *(Exiting indoors)* Him.

Doyle Good day. Was that our earnest postmistress I saw hurrying away just now?

Annie Yes sir, it's her half day.

Doyle Then I hope you are equally qualified to send wires.

Annie I am sir. Fully trained now.

Doyle Good. I have three here—one of them is quite long I'm afraid. To my publisher.

He hands them to her

Annie Shall I do the short ones first, sir? Let's just make sure I can read them. *(Starts to read the first)* This GBS—is it a place?

Doyle *(Laughs)* No, it's George Bernard Shaw. You may remember him—Mr Shaw—lived here in the village until last year—red beard, on a crutch, always talking. The recipient will understand well enough who I mean just by the initials.

The lights fade on the scene

Scene 20

On Ludshott Common, soon after

Flora, Richard and Mavis walk, the girls either side on Richard's arms

Flora Remember the first day you came into the post office, Richard, and I sold you a post card?

Richard Very well. I had to write home and tell mother I'd arrived safely.

Mavis And I remember being at home with her when she received it.

Flora The view you chose was taken from about here, I should think.

Richard Yes, I believe you're right.

Mavis But listen to the birds, and smell the heather! They weren't on the post card!

Richard It's magnificent! And what are those blue hills in the distance?

Flora The South Downs—see that gap?—it's where the turnpike to Portsmouth goes through. D'you know, one of the men in the village actually rode his 'penny-farthing' there and back in a day, a few years ago?

Richard Never!

Flora And over there—see those other hills, nearer?—that's Selborne hanger, where Gilbert White the naturalist lived.

Mavis You seem to know everything, Flora.

Richard What's that large patch of red blight among the heather over there?

Flora Ah, that's dodder. It's a parasite and drags the plants around it down to earth.

Mavis How gruesome!

Flora If I were a novelist, I'd write a book called 'Dodder'.

Richard You would? Why?

Flora It would be the story of a man or a woman—probably a woman—of a fine, sensitive nature, married to someone who was strong, coarse and encroaching by nature.

Mavis The dodder!

Flora I would tell how, in time, the heather person shrank and withered, while the dodder one fattened and prospered.

Richard The villain of the piece.

Flora No! The dodder cannot help being dodder—it was made that way. The dodder man has no evil intentions—he may even be kindly disposed. It just happens that his presence ruins the heather.

Mavis He thrives and becomes more and more bumptious and important …

Richard Probably a stockbroker, with a white waistcoat and a thick gold watch-chain.

Mavis A well-respected man in society circles.

Flora While she, on the other hand, just withers away into a wraith of a woman.

Richard Jolly fine. I shall write this story.

Mavis You shall not! This is Flora's story.

Richard *(A little hurt)* You don't think I can handle such a delicate tale?

Mavis Flora knows all about people.

Flora I'm not sure I do. I've been told I prefer places to people.

Richard *(Seizing her hand)* Nonsense, you shall do it*! (Swinging her round in a waltz)* Flora knows about it all. She knows! She knows!

Mavis *(Laughing)* Richard! Stop it—what will people think?

Richard But there's no-one around, is there. There's no-one for miles around.

> *Bob Pikesley enters and looks at the dancing couple blankly –*
> *Flora suddenly sees him and stops in embarrassment*

Flora Oh—hello Bob.

Bob Pikesley A'ternoon.

Flora We were just—admiring the view from here.

Bob Pikesley I see.

Flora These are friends of mine—from London.

Bob Pikesley Oh ar.

Flora Richard and Mavis.

Bob Pikesley Pleased to meet 'ee.

Flora We were going up to the pine clump.

Bob Pikesley Be rain afore you get back.

Flora Surely not.

Bob Pikesley Same as before.

Flora But there's not a cloud in the sky.

Bob Pikesley See if I'm not right. *(He walks past them to exit)* Helpless crittur!

Richard Who was he?

Flora Bob Pikesley. He keeps cows down in the valley. Lives with his sister.

Mavis Sounds like he's the local weather prophet too.

Flora I've never known him wrong yet. Perhaps we'd better get on.

Richard 'Some are weather-wise, some are otherwise.'

Flora Who's that?

Richard Benjamin Franklin.

Mavis Don't say Richard's found someone you haven't read, Flora.

Flora I don't live among the bookshops in London like you do. I have to rely on Madame Warr's lending library across the road.

Richard Then why not come to live in London?

Mavis Yes, why not?

Richard Think of all the theatres and museums we could visit.

Mavis And the picture galleries—you'd love those.

Richard And the country outings on Sundays.

Flora But I'm already in the country. And what would I do for work?

Mavis Oh, we could find you work, couldn't we Richard.

Flora I've no qualifications—nothing on paper.

Richard A correspondence course—with the Civil Service college—that's what you need. Only a guinea, and you'd pass the examinations with flying colours.

Flora With my education? Do you think so?

Mavis You pick things up so quickly.

Richard I'm certain. I'll make a point of sending you the papers on it when we get home.

Flora I'm not sure.

Mavis You'll love it in London, Flora. *(She starts coughing)* Oh, excuse me.

Richard I thought you'd lost that cough.

Mavis So did I. *(Coughing again)*

Flora Mavis, are you all right?

Richard She's had it for a while. I thought the fresh air out here had cured it.

Flora It's probably the smell from that patch of burnt heather over there. It can catch in your throat sometimes.

Richard You're probably right.

Mavis *(Only slightly recovered)* I'm better now.

Richard We'd better get back to the house. Early start tomorrow.

Flora Back to London.

Richard Back to the city smoke. Until our next weekend off.

Flora When will that be?

Richard Not too long, I hope. But before that, you must visit us. You don't know what you're missing if you've never seen the city.

Mavis Yes, really Flora.

Flora *(Dubious)* Well—I'll see if Mr Chapman can give me time off.

Richard It's decided then. You've shown us the wonders of the country-side, and we shall show you the marvels of the city.

As the three exit arm in arm

We'll ride along gas-lit streets on top of a bus …

Mavis Eat roast chestnuts and look in all the shop windows …

Richard Show you the Central Telegraph Office in Threadneedle Street, where all your messages come from …

Flora Oh yes, "T.S." we call it.

Mavis And take you to … *(Coughing again)* Oh dear, I do wish I could get rid of this silly cough. It's so embarrassing.

Scene 21

In Crossways Road, Grayshott

Walter and Ernest Chapman meet

Ernest Chapman Good morning to you, brother. Are you well?

Walter Chapman Never felt better, Ernest.

Ernest Chapman Glad to hear it.

Walter Chapman You sound unsure.

Ernest Chapman No, no—I am sure. I am glad to hear that you say you are well.

Walter Chapman But I still sense a reservation in your voice.

Ernest Chapman You do?

Walter Chapman Let me assure you. The problems of the past are over. I am at peace with myself.

Ernest Chapman It is not I who need the assurance—it is your wife. Emily is convinced her life is at risk if she comes back to you. Not to mention the children.

Walter Chapman She has a vivid imagination, brother.

Ernest Chapman Oh, she has no need to imagine. If a quarter of the things she says are true, she has no need to imagine. How can she be sure this peace will last?

Walter Chapman It will last. Trade is good—I am healthy—I am content. I am respected in the community, am I not?

Ernest Chapman For your skills in carpentry, there is no-one your equal in the area.

Walter Chapman My work is even in the church. The new altar.

Ernest Chapman Then you are truly Established in your carpentry. But what has Dr Lyndon to say about your physical situation?

Walter Chapman What should he have to say? A healthy man has no need of a physician.

Ernest Chapman Indeed. But I would be happier to hear the physician say so.

Walter Chapman Then you had better ask Dr Lyndon yourself. As far as I am concerned, I have no reason to waste his time with a visit. Ah, it must be Tuesday—here's the man from the *Herald*.

Ernest Chapman You do not convince me, brother.

Walter Chapman No? But he comes searching for news every week at this time.

Ernest Chapman That's not what I meant, as well you know. I am concerned to know if your wife and children can safely return home now.

William Sillick approaches

Sillick Good morning, gentlemen.

Ernest Chapman *(Sharply)* Morning, Sillick. *(To Walter)* Well, we shall talk more of this.

Walter Chapman You are concerning yourself over nothing. There is no problem.

Ernest Chapman I hope to God you are right. *(To Sillick)* Good day. Mr Sillick.

Ernest departs

Sillick Have I interrupted a family meeting?

Walter Chapman My brother Ernest was enquiring after my health, that is all.

Sillick I see.

Walter Chapman Which is excellent. Excellent. And now you are here to see Miss Timms?

Sillick Ah—

Walter Chapman You do not imagine that I was unaware of the particular interest you take in my employee?

Sillick An entirely innocent relationship, Mr Chapman, I assure you.

Walter Chapman Yes. Maybe. She does seem to attract unusual friends. Not entirely appropriate for a person with her—responsibilities.

Sillick I'm sorry if …

Walter Chapman Do not encourage her to tell you things which are—better left undisclosed.

Sillick Indeed not. I fully respect the confidential nature of her job.

Walter Chapman Her job—yes. Yes, her job.

Sillick I assumed that was what you were referring to.

Walter Chapman Her position—in the post office. Yes. It has been… It is… We must naturally uphold the regulations—as laid down by the postmaster-general.

Sillick I fully understand that, Mr Chapman.

Walter Chapman Good. Good.

Sillick Have no fear—I am the model of discretion in my reporting of such affairs.

Scene 22

Mrs Parkhurst's house, some weeks later

Mrs Parkhurst is doing housework as Flora enters

Flora I'm home, Mrs Parkhurst. You're busy as ever, I see.

Mrs Parkhurst Seven children at home and a husband to look after, young Flora—doesn't give you much time for yourself.

Flora You must feel tired.

Mrs Parkhurst I do. I don't believe I've sat down a moment all day, except for meals. And the minister came over to see us today, since we never get to see him at the chapel in town—so that was extra work.

Flora I hope the children were good.

Mrs Parkhurst They were good, and well they might be. He insisted on having them share the dish of cakes I'd made for his tea.

Flora Oh dear.

Mrs Parkhurst 'Suffer the little children to come unto me,' he said—then he blessed them all and sent them off to play.

Flora Ah.

Mrs Parkhurst But I was glad he came. Mr Parkhurst will see him on Sunday, being as how it's one of his Chapel Sundays, but I wanted to tell him first.

Flora I see. *(Uncertainly)* Tell him what?

Mrs Parkhurst Well you'd better know, for it'll be obvious soon enough. I did think I'd done with it all, at my time of life, but—I'm expecting again.

Flora *(Not sure what to say)* Oh.

Mrs Parkhurst I know it's God's will and I must be patient—but I do dread it starting to show. All the clothes I had are either worn out or given away. And where we'll find the money to buy new, I just don't know. Mr Parkhurst, bless him, has never had a day out of work in his life, but … *(She is near to tears)*

Flora I'm sure you'll cope. *(Trying to return to normality)* I bought you the things you asked for in the village.

Mrs Parkhurst That's very good of you, dear. You're a great help to me.

Flora It's all right. I'll be in my room if you need me.

Flora tries to exit, but Mrs Parkhurst holds her in conversation

Mrs Parkhurst I remember when I was your age. We lived over by Selborne then. You and your walking—you should see the Hanger at Selborne when the primroses are out! And the hop-picking season—the whole family would pack up and go off in the donkey-cart to Farnham, bag and baggage, leaving grandmother at home to look after the animals. 'Twas a regular holiday for us children—happiest days of my life.

Flora It sounds wonderful.

Mrs Parkhurst Mind, it was hard work during the day, but we had plenty of fun in the evenings. Now all this riff-raff from the towns does it, and nobody who thinks themselves respectable goes any more.

Flora What a shame.

Mrs Parkhurst Used to shut the schools for us to go hop-picking, they did—but not now—times have changed. Well, I must get Mr Parkhurst's tea ready for him. There's a fire lit in your room and I'll bring the supper tray up at the usual time.

Flora Thank you—that's very kind.

Mrs Parkhurst You'll not be going out tonight?

Flora No, I have some books to read.

Mrs Parkhurst I'm not sure what's worse—going out with the wrong people or not going out at all. Still, one day you'll be married and then you'll learn what's what.

Flora smiles thinly at her and exits—the lights fade on the scene

Scene 23

In Grayshott Post Office, some time later

Annie is on duty—Isobel has come in for a chat

Isobel Annie, have you heard? You missed such a scene yesterday—with Millie.

Annie *(Sorting mail and not paying full attention)* No, Izzy, I haven't—what's Millie been up to?

Isobel It's her Sam—he's jilted her—can you imagine?

Annie Sam? I didn't think he had it in him.

Isobel Oh that's not fair, Annie. Poor Millie's heartbroken.

Annie 'Better a bad husband than no husband at all,' as they say.

Isobel We were all there, trying to console her—she was borrowing handkerchiefs from everybody …

Annie Sounds a bit unhygienic.

Isobel Then suddenly she jumped up, threw her handkerchief away …

Annie Whose handkerchief?

Isobel Listen, this is serious—she jumped up and shouted, 'I'll make him suffer for this—I'll breach him!—I'll breach him!'

Annie She's been reading too many newspapers. People are bringing breach-of-promise cases just to sell the story these days.

Isobel Annie, you're being unromantic.

Annie Well I don't suppose Sam even *made* a promise.

Isobel You don't go around with a man unless he's promised to you, do you. Or at least <u>we</u> don't.

Walter Chapman enters from the house, with woodworking tools in hand

Annie Now then, Isobel, did you want some stamps?

Isobel Stamps? *(Sees Walter and understands)* Oh, no—no, thank you.

Annie I'll probably see you on Saturday then, at the dance—with Arthur.

Isobel Yes, I expect so. Thank you. I'll see you there, then. Goodbye. *(She exits)*

Walter Chapman Miss Symonds.

Annie Yes, Mr Chapman.

Walter Chapman I must see Miss Timms as soon as she arrives.

Annie I'll tell her as soon as she gets here—she shouldn't be long. Can I say what it's about?

Walter Chapman A private matter, Miss Symonds, a private matter. *(Hissing)* T'were well it were done quickly. *(To Annie)* Have we been busy today?

Annie Yes, fairly busy.

Walter Chapman Good, good. Let us hope then. Let us hope. *(He exits to the house)*

Annie *(To herself)* What on earth's all that about? *(The telegraph starts to tinkle)* Oh bother—the telegraph. *(She goes to it)* Message from 'T. S.'

Flora enters from the street while Annie is off transcribing the message

Flora *(Calls to Annie as she takes off her coat and hat)* Is that today's war report coming in?

Annie *(Off)* No, it's not.

Flora *(Listening to the tinkling of the message)* It just said 'HINDHEAD'.

Annie *(Off)* Yes—it's about the new office there. Addressed to Mr Chapman.

Flora What does it say?

The message stops, and Annie emerges

Annie You'd better read it. *(Hands the message sheet to Flora)*

Flora *(Reading)* I see—I suppose it was predictable.

Annie Does it mean you'll have to leave? That would be terrible.

Flora Most of our customers come from Hindhead. Once there's a telegraph office there …

Annie Can't you apply to work in it? That wouldn't mean moving.

Flora We'll have to see. I'd better put this in an envelope and take it to Mr Chapman.

Annie And try to pretend we haven't seen it! Silly isn't it? Oh, he wanted to see you anyway, as soon as you arrived.

Flora Probably about the same thing. It says 'further to our recent letter.'

Annie Good luck then. He was whispering bits from Macbeth when he asked for you.

Flora Something ominous, like 'Toil and trouble'?

Annie No, not that exactly—but there aren't any <u>good</u> bits in Macbeth, are there.

Flora smiles at her and exits to the house

'Double, double, toil and trouble;'
'Fire burn and cauldron bubble.'
'When shall we three meet again?'

Richard enters to hear this

Richard 'In thunder, lightning, or in rain?'

Annie Very appropriate, Richard. You sound how I feel.

Richard Have I arrived at a bad time? I was hoping for a quiet word with Flora.

Annie She's having a 'quiet word' with Mr Chapman at the moment.

Richard Nothing serious, I hope.

Annie Nothing she's done, if that's what you mean.

Richard That's a relief anyway. How long will she be?

Annie How long is a piece of post office string?

Richard With or without sealing wax?

Annie That's better—at least you're smiling now.

Richard I confess I don't feel like it.

Annie You too? Bad news?

Richard I thought I'd better come and tell Flora in person.

Annie Oh dear—what's that?

Flora enters

Flora Richard! I wasn't expecting you here again so soon. *(She goes to him. They almost embrace—Flora senses his mood)* Is there something …?

Richard *(Confidentially)* Can we find somewhere to talk?

Flora Well, not at my lodgings—my room's got a bed in it, and that would never do.

Richard *(Half laughing)* No—no it wouldn't, would it.

Flora We could take a walk down the street, to the turnpike. There's not too many people about at the moment.

(To Annie) Can you look after the office for a few minutes, Annie?

Annie I might as well get used to it.

Flora grabs her coat & hat again—she and Richard exit to the street.

Telegram boys enter from inside

Willie *(mimicking Flora)* … that would never do!

Alf D'you think that's what she says to Bob Pikesley too?

Willie Bob Pikesley wouldn't know what she was talking about.

Annie And neither do you. I've told you before—out of the office unless you're called.

Willie Yes, Miss Symonds.

Alf Didn't something come in just now?

Annie Nothing that needs delivering. Now be off with you.

Willie But we've been waiting for ages with nothing to do. *(Boys exit to room)*

Annie *(Calling after them)* Seems you'll have even less to do when Hindhead opens.

Scene 24

In Crossways Road, immediately after

Flora and Richard promenade during this scene

Richard What did she mean, 'might as well get used to it'?

Flora Oh, I'll tell you later. How's Mavis?

Richard That's one of the things I came to tell you about—she's not at all well.

Flora The cough?

Richard The doctor couldn't be sure, but he suspects tuberculosis.

Flora Oh, Richard, I am sorry. Poor Mavis.

Richard He says she shouldn't stay in London this winter.

Flora Just as she was doing so well in her new job too. Isn't she frightened?

Richard Disappointed—not frightened. She's certain the doctor's made a mistake.

Flora But you don't think so.

Richard *(Shakes his head grimly. Then, half laughing)* He wondered if she could be moved to the South of France for a while.

Flora Your poor mother could never afford that.

Richard Of course not. Bournemouth is the best we can manage.

Flora I see.

Richard At first she flatly refused to be 'packed off' as she called it.

Flora But she <u>is</u> going?

Richard Of course she is. These things are taken seriously today. We've told her she must stay in a sanatorium there until she's cured.

Flora But the money.

Richard Our Aunt Maggie has a friend there—a trained nurse. Mavis can stay with her for three months. We'll find the money for that.

Flora And then?

Richard Then? By then it will be Spring.

There is a silence

Flora And you came down from London especially to tell me this. It was good of you.

Richard Not just that. *(Pause)* I also wanted to say it may be some time before I see you again, Flora. With Mavis so ill …

Flora She must be your first priority, of course.

Richard There'll be no holidays for me, not even weekends, until she's better. And what with mother to look after as well …

Flora Poor Richard.

Richard Poor in every sense, I'm afraid. One day you'll read in the news-papers, "Young man in moneylender's clutches," and you'll find you know him.

Flora I shall not—you've far more sense than that.

Richard I hope so—but at the moment I feel as if I'm trying to climb out of a pit—and I keep getting knocked back down again just when I'm at the top.

Flora Things are sure to get better. "Never flinch"—remember?

Richard Flinch? I wish I had your good country wisdom to fall back on. I feel it will always be like this for me from now on—I can't see an end to it.

Flora Richard …

Richard I can never marry you—you know that, don't you Flora?

Flora Marry?

Richard Not while I have to borrow money just to live.

Flora *(Hurt, but not flinching)* But—you don't want to marry anyone, do you? And perhaps by the time you do you'll have made a fortune.

Richard Flora, I didn't mean …

Flora It's all right, Richard. I understand.

Richard I didn't mean it that way.

Flora You must keep an eye on the time. Which train are you getting back?

Richard Five minutes past the hour. Look, I'm …

Flora Then you should be going. It's a long walk to the station.

Richard Yes. Yes—I'll write of course—and so will Mavis.

Flora And I shall write back.

Richard Thank you—I'll appreciate that. Well—goodbye then, Flora.

Flora Goodbye, Richard.

They hold hands for a while at arms length, then Richard turns and walks off.

Flora *(Softly, after him)* Goodbye.

> *Flora waits, looking where he has gone.*
> *Suddenly he returns, but stops before reaching her.*

Richard Goodbye, Flora.

> *He thinks of holding her, then turns and hurries off again*

Flora And I never even told him <u>my</u> news.

> *Flora turns and exits in the opposite direction*

Scene 25

In Grayshott Post Office, at the same time

Annie is still on duty. Walter Chapman enters

Walter Chapman Has Miss Timms left?

Annie She's out—handling a customer's enquiry, Mr Chapman.

Walter Chapman I see. *(Hissing)* To him that hath shall be given. *(To Annie)* She has no doubt informed you of the forthcoming changes.

Annie Hindhead, you mean.

Walter Chapman It is most unlikely that the remaining telegraph traffic will warrant retaining two staff here. I have advised Miss Timms to look elsewhere for employment.

Annie She'll be sorry to go.

Walter Chapman She at least has no roots in this village as you have, Miss Symonds. I am sure she will find her feet equally well in another location. Yes. *(Pause)* Now I must see to the house. My wife is returning with the children this evening.

Annie *(In surprise)* Mrs Chapman?

Walter Chapman Yes. They have been too long away. Far too long. *(Hissing as he exits)* Vengeance is mine, saith the Lord.

Scene 26

In Crossways Road, Grayshott

Winifred Storr and "Gee" Leuchars are walking in the street

Winifred Mr Terry came over last night and taught mother how to ride her new bicycle.

Gee How did he do that?

Winifred Put a broomstick through under the saddle and used it to steer her round the garden.

Gee What fun! My mother hasn't dared try yet. Your family always gets to do things first—you've got one of those Kodaks now, haven't you?

Winifred I'll take a snap-shot of you if you like. You can pose for me.

Gee Not me!

Winifred Famous member of the local girls cricket team.

Gee Just because you beat us last week!

Winifred And you had Mary Doyle on your side too.

Gee So?

Winifred Her father plays cricket almost better than he writes books.

Gee I got more runs than she did.

Winifred The whole team only got 17 runs!

Gee Anyway, Mr Whitaker's offered us his gardens for practice next Saturday, and strawberries and cream afterwards.

Winifred You need it. *Mrs* Whitaker brought three brace of partridges round to us the other day.

Gee Perhaps she thinks you're starving poor …

Winifred Starving? You should see the spread our mother put out when Miss James came round for tea last week.

Gee *(Carrying on her teasing)* You'll all be in the workhouse before you know it.

Winifred *(Ignoring her)* And I played the piano to her. She said I was very good.

Gee Better than my sister on the violin, I hope.

Winifred I'm going up to London with mother for a lesson tomorrow.

Gee Which train?

Winifred The eleven o'clock.

Gee I'll be on that too.

Winifred Will you? Where are you going—anywhere exciting?

Gee To the dentist!

Winifred Oh, poor Gee!

Gee I'll bring a good book with me.

Winifred Me too. What are you reading now?

Gee 'A Desert Drama,' by you-know-who.

Both *(Together)* A. Conan Doyle.

They exit, still talking

Scene 27

By the new Hindhead Post Office

William Sillick and Conan Doyle enter

Sillick Well, Mr Doyle, how do you like the new telegraph office here? I should think you could pop over and back while your breakfast egg is boiling now.

Doyle It is certainly more convenient.

Sillick Could hardly be closer.

Doyle Have to get used to the new staff, of course. And no more teasing the young Grayshott postmistress.

Sillick Miss Timms? She's not transferring up here then? She hadn't told me.

Doyle Apparently not. An interesting lady that.

Sillick Yes—You think so?

Doyle Not much conversation, at least not with me, yet one perceives a certain depth of spirit within her.

Sillick Well, that is your line of business is it not—the spirit world?

Doyle A certain feeling of—mystery.

Sillick A case for Holmes to solve perhaps.

Doyle I do write other works you know, Mr Sillick.

Lights fade

Scene 28

Mrs Parkhurst's house, some days later

The baby has arrived—Flora gets her first look

Flora She's lovely. What are you calling her?

Mrs Parkhurst Elsie. She's my little Lammas lamb.

Flora Hello, Elsie.

Mrs Parkhurst There, there. You'll have some nicey-picey dilly-dilly-water in a min-min when brother Herbie comes back from the chemie.

Flora Mr Parkhurst tells me you didn't have an easy time.

Mrs Parkhurst Two doctors and the district nurse—and the chloroform. But I kept telling myself, "I know my redeemer liveth," and *(to the baby)* you were no trouble in the end, were you. No you weren't.

Flora What do the other children think of her?

Mrs Parkhurst *(To the baby)* They love you, don't they. Yes they do. And big sister Mabel's going to give you a nice bathie-pathie when she gets homie-pomie, isn't she.

Flora It's nice to see you taking a rest for once.

Mrs Parkhurst First I've had since Ivy was born eight years ago, and I mean to make the most of it, I can tell you. It's the last I'll get of this sort. *(To the baby)* Yes, you're the last—there won't be any more like you, will there. Oh no there won't. *(To Flora)* I'll make sure of that.

Flora *(A little embarrassed, just smiles and nods)*

Mrs Parkhurst So you're leaving Grayshott soon. Where are you going?

Flora I don't know yet. I'm looking for a vacancy at another post office.

Mrs Parkhurst Still want to be a working girl, then. Not settling down to get married—and have babies of your own.

Flora I haven't found 'Mr Right' yet.

Mrs Parkhurst What happened to that Richard?

Flora Oh—we keep in touch.

Lights fade

Scene 29

In Grayshott Post Office, a few days later

Annie is on duty—Emily Chapman is with her

Annie I'm glad you're here for Flora's last day, Mrs Chapman.

Emily Chapman *(Pensively)* Yes. I wonder what memories Grayshott will have for her.

Annie Oh, I think she's enjoyed it here. Different to anywhere she's been before, she says.

Emily Chapman Different. I imagine it has been.

Annie All the hills and heather—she grew up among clay and cornfields— 'lark rise' country she called it. I remember her telling me once the air round here went to her head like wine.

Emily Chapman I wonder. Did she also tell you why she left the lodgings she had with us here?

Annie *(A little embarrassed)* No, she never did.

Emily Chapman Not a hint?

Annie No—she never told me, and I never asked.

Emily Chapman I see. *(A pause)* Has she heard any news of her brother yet?

Annie Edwin? He's still posted as 'missing.' She must be worried, but she doesn't let it show.

Emily Chapman 'Never flinch.'

Annie You've heard her say that too.

Emily Chapman I've had reason to remember it these last few months.

Lights fade

Scene 30

Farewells in Grayshott

Flora moves from character to character around the 'stage'.

Marion is twirling a bag of sweets closed for Flora to take away with her

Marion It won't be the same without you, Flora.

Flora Nor you, Marion. I'm sure Annie will help you with any more speeches you have to make.

Marion Oh, they say it's not going to be my turn now for ages. *(Pensively)* I hope they liked the one I did.

Flora I'm sure they loved it.

Marion *(Handing her the sweets)* These are to keep you going on the train journey.

Flora Thank you—it's quite a long way. *(Looking for her purse)* How much are they?

Marion Flora! They're a present.

Flora That's very kind. I'll remember you with each sweet I eat.

Marion Just so long as you also remember me when you're rich and famous.

Flora *(Laughing)* And the moon turns blue and all the rivers run uphill. Goodbye Marion.

Marion Goodbye Flora. Bless you.

Flora Alf and Willie—my two best messenger boys.

Alf You going far?

Flora To Bournemouth.

Willie That's by the seaside, isn't it?

Flora Yes, the seaside—another new experience for me.
    Goodbye, Mr Chapman. It was very kind of you to take me on here.

Walter Chapman *(Carrying his carpenter's tools)* Goodbye, Miss Timms. *(Hissing)* Yes, parting is such sweet sorrow.

Flora Mrs Chapman.

Emily Chapman Flora—I'm … *(shakes her head, near tears)* I'm sorry …

Flora There's no need, Mrs Chapman. Give my love to the children.

Emily Chapman Love? Yes, of course.

Flora Bob. Bob Pikesley!

Bob Pikesley They tells me you're a'going.

Flora Yes. I'm just off to the station.

Bob Pikesley On your two feet.

Flora It's the way I arrived, and it's the way I want to leave. The carter's taken my luggage.

Bob Pikesley Rain before you get there.

Flora I have my hat and coat.

Bob Pikesley Helpless crittur.

Flora Goodbye Mrs Parkhurst.

Mrs Parkhurst We'll meet again one day, I'm sure of that.

Flora I wish I was.

Mrs Parkhurst When Elsie's a grown girl, you've got children of your own, and I'm a grandmother several times over—we'll meet again.

Flora Goodbye Izzy. That's a lovely present you bought me. *(They embrace)*

Isobel I hope you like it—it's supposed to bring you luck.

Flora It will—I'm sure of it. And Annie. *(They embrace too)*

Annie *(A little tearfully)* Best-trained telegraph operator in the land.

Flora I'd have gone 'barmy on the crumpet' without you. Ly-ces-ter, War-ces-ter, Has-le-merry!

Annie You'll write, won't you.

Flora I might even send you a message on the telegraph.

Annie An electric letter!

Flora Keep writing the poetry.

Annie Oh, it's you that's the writer, not me.

Flora I wish I could believe that. Goodbye, Annie.

Flora is now alone

Goodbye Grayshott—heathery Grayshott. I came to you as a young girl of twenty-one, and I leave you nearly three years older—but any wiser? Perhaps Bob Pikesley's right—I'm a 'helpless crittur.' There's Annie and Izzy and the rest of them rushing to get married—but me? Coming up for my quarter century, and still on the shelf.

This is where I said goodbye to Richard—for the last time. I wonder if he'll ever— Or did he really not want to marry anyone? Who knows? Perhaps you're right dear Mr Foreshaw. 'He rides swiftest who rides alone.' There must be worse things in life than being single.

Come on now Flora, best foot forward—it's three miles to the station and you can beat the carter there yet. *(She exits)*

Scene 31

Inside the Chapmans' accommodation at Grayshott Post Office

We hear Emily Chapman scream

Walter Chapman Whore, strumpet!

He holds a carpenter's chisel—there is blood on it and on him

Emily Chapman Walter—the baby! No!!

Walter Chapman *(Stabbing her repeatedly)* Your baby—not my baby—not Letty's baby.

He stabs her again

Emily Chapman *(Last gasp)* Walter!

Walter Chapman God forgive me—vengeance is mine, saith the Lord.

Ernest Chapman rushes in

Ernest Chapman Brother, what have you done here?

He brushes Walter away and bends over Emily

Emily, can you hear me? *(To Annie off)* Fetch Dr Lyndon, and hurry.

I fear we are too late. Why did you do this, brother? You had no business to send her into Eternity.

Walter Chapman She was here in Letty's place.

Ernest Chapman If only you had lived in the love of God... It is your disbelief that has brought you to this sorry state.

Walter Chapman Why did she do it to me?

Ernest Chapman May God have mercy on your soul. Only the blood of Jesus will save you now.

Walter Chapman Why did she leave me? Why? Why?

Scene 32

Epilogue

Sillick The funeral of the late Mrs Chapman took place on Thursday afternoon, and was the occasion for an extraordinary manifestation of sympathy, this terrible tragedy having been the one topic of conversation in the whole neighbourhood during the week.

Ernest Walter was remanded to the next Winchester Assizes. At the trial he pleaded guilty to manslaughter, but on the request of his Counsel a plea of "Not guilty" was entered.

Sillick Dr. Worthington, medical superintendent of Hampshire County Asylum, reported that in his opinion the prisoner was insane at the time of the crime.

Ernest The jury returned a verdict of guilty but not responsible at law for his action. The judge ordered Walter to be detained during His Majesty's pleasure.

Flora Mr Chapman spent the rest of his life in Broadmoor. I often pictured him there, sitting with his head in his hands—as according to the newspaper reports he'd done throughout his trial.

Ernest Later he recovered his reason sufficiently to be allowed to work at his trade in the prison workshop—a white-haired old man, harmless and happy in his work. Much that had passed had been wiped from his memory, but he still had his delusions—and one of these was that his wife came frequently to visit him. She, poor soul, was at rest.

Scene 33

Flora's Wedding — 7th January 1903, at Twickenham

John Thompson is waiting at the altar, his back to the audience. The Wedding March starts—'Flora' appears in wedding dress, walking slowly down the aisle.

Our character Flora views the scene.

Flora It's a wedding! But whose wedding? I don't recognise the man—the girl looks familiar. My height, my build, my features, my walk … Mercy, it <u>is</u> me! My wedding. So I <u>am</u> to get married. But who to? It's not Richard—he's tall and well-built—this one's shorter, almost portly. And who's giving me away?—I can't quite make out. Not my father. Is Edwin there?—I feel sure he survived in South Africa, but I can't see him either. There seems to be nobody I know—but it <u>is</u> me.

So—Mrs Parkhurst, poor Mrs Chapman, dear Annie—I am to follow you down the aisle after all. Better a bad husband than no husband at all? But why should I think him bad? The dodder man—he has no evil intentions— he may even be kindly disposed. It just happens—that his presence stifles the heather person....

Never flinch, Flora. Remember, we are as we are made, and that's the end of it.

She takes the place of the bride in the aisle, and walks down to stand by John Thompson. The music swells as she does so, and they walk offstage together, away from the audience

— THE END —

Flora's Peverel

Second part of 'Flora Thompson: Beyond Candleford'

Flora Thompson in Liphook 1916–1928

Flora came to Liphook in 1916 at the age of 39, when her husband John was appointed there as Postmaster. It was fifteen years since she had left the neighbouring village of Grayshott (her 'Heatherley') as a single girl, having herself worked as Assistant Postmistress there for nearly three years.

The Thompsons stayed in Liphook for twelve years, during which time their third child was born and Flora started to write more seriously than she had before.

She wrote no book like 'Heatherley' about this period of her life, but there is a large volume of her nature notes and other similar writings from which to piece together the background to her time in Liphook. Added to these notes, we have the historical records of the village and some verbatim memories from those who were still alive who remember the Thompson family.

True to her habit of fictionalising the names of real places and people, she gave the name 'Peverel' to Weavers Down, a favourite heath of hers which rises to the west of Liphook. She used this name in the title both of her published collection of nature notes ('The Peverel Papers') and the postal writers circle (the 'Peverel Society') which she started during this time.

For ten years the Thompsons lived in rented post office accommodation in the middle of the village, until they finally bought a home of their own – a house recently built at the very foot of Flora's beloved 'Peverel Down.' However her joy at this was to be short-lived, as her husband almost immediately applied for, and obtained, a promotion in Devonshire. She left Hampshire with a heavy heart, this time never to return.

Flora's Peverel

Act 1 – 1916–18

Prelude: Flanders, April 1916

Scene 1: Flora's garden in Bournemouth, April 1916

Scene 2: Canadian army camp, near Liphook, September 1916

Scene 3: Liphook Post Office, later that morning

Scene 4: Lynchmere Common

Scene 5: Flora's room, Liphook Post Office

Scene 6: On the road from Forest Mere

Scene 7: The Postmaster's House, soon after

Scene 8: On the Road with Maggie Tidy

Scene 9: Liphook Post Office, summer 1917

Scene 10: On Bramshott Common, later that day

Scene 11: Liphook Post Office, soon after

Scene 12: On the Road with Bill & Maggie Tidy

Scene 13: Flora's room, Liphook Post Office, early 1918

Scene 14: A street in Liphook, at the same time

Scene 15: Flora's room, Liphook Post Office, at the same time

Scene 16: Split scene – Flora and Louie

—INTERVAL—
Advertisement for Correspondence Courses, 1925

Act 2 – 1926–28

Scene 17: An open space near Liphook, summer 1926

Scene 18: Liphook Post Office, a few days later

Scene 19: In the garden of the Postmaster's house, a few weeks later

Scene 20: Liphook Post Office, at the same time

Scene 21: On Weavers Down soon after

Scene 22: The Leggett's farm, Griggs Green, a few weeks later

Scene 23: 'Woolmer Gate', Griggs Green, soon after

Scene 24: Liphook Post Office, early morning a few weeks later

Scene 25: Weavers Down, early spring 1927

Scene 26: The Telephone Exchange, Liphook Post Office

Scene 27: 'Woolmer Gate', Griggs Green, soon after
Scene 28: Lynchmere Common
Scene 29: The Leggett's farm, Griggs Green, a few weeks later
Scene 30: Hewshott House, Liphook, summer 1927
Scene 31: 'Woolmer Gate', Griggs Green, some time later
Scene 32: 'Woolmer Gate', Griggs Green, autumn 1928
Scene 33: April 1937
Scene 34: May 1947

Cast (ages: 1916–1928)

Postman (at Bournemouth)
Flora Thompson (39–51 and 60 in 1937)
John Thompson (42–54 and 73 in 1947)
'Louie' Woods (19)
Sergeant John Mumford (24)
Harry Envis – a postman (30s)
'Joe' Leggett (8 in 1916)
Bill Tidy – a tinker (say 60s)
Maggie Tidy, his wife (say 60s)
Dr Ronald Campbell Macfie (50)
Corporal (say 30s)
Two Canadian soldiers (say 20s)
Gypsy woman – (spry late 80s)
Mrs Parkhurst from 'Heatherley' (62)
Elsie Parkhurst, her youngest daughter (18)
Winifred ('Diana') Thompson (22)
Peter Thompson (8 in Oct 1926)
'Joe' Leggett (18 in 1926)
Eileen Leggett (16)
Mrs Leggett, their mother – Irish (51)
Capt. Byfield (60s?)
Sam the shepherd (70s?)
Chairman of cable company (60s)
Peter Thompson (18 in March 1937)
Richard Brownlow (60, non-speaking)

Flora's Peverel

Prelude Scene in Flanders, April 1916

A Blackout – 'Keep the Home Fires Burning' is played hesitantly on a harmonica. There are flashes and the sound of gunfire – after which, silence.

Scene 1

Flora's garden in Bournemouth, April 1916

The postman arrives and greets Flora

Postman Morning, Mrs Thompson – lovely day again. Can even start to believe it's spring, can't you.

Flora Yes, you can. And all the better for having the children up and about again.

Postman Thought I hadn't seen them around lately. Been ill, have they?

Flora Whooping cough, both of them. We had to miss seeing my brother last month because of it – when he was home on leave.

Postman Never mind – this weather'll soon put roses in their cheeks, won't it?

Flora Let's hope so.

Postman *(Hands he some letters)* Three for you today.

Flora Thank you.

Postman If I get my round done in time, you know, I fancy I'll do a spot of gardening this afternoon. Could do with a bit of a work-over after all that late snow we've had. Kept me indoors most of last month, it did, and … Are you all right, Mrs Thompson?

Flora is holding a returned letter she had sent to her brother

Mrs Thompson?

Flora *(Flatly)* Edwin – killed in action.

Postman Your brother?

Flora My brother. My closest brother. The one we missed seeing. Now we'll never see him again. Ever.

76

Scene 2

Canadian army camp, near Liphook, September 1916

'Louie' Woods is delivering mail on her bicycle
– Sgt John Mumford walks across her path

Louie Hey, watch where you're going!

Sgt Mumford Sorry ma'am – too early in the morning for me – I'm still half asleep.

Louie All right for some – I have to be up before sunrise to get your post delivered.

Sgt Mumford And much appreciated too. Anything for Sgt John Mumford there?

Louie Goodness, *I* don't know. It's already sorted by the time I pick it up. The postmaster's wife gets up at four o'clock to do that.

Sgt Mumford Can't accuse you British of oversleeping.

Louie Not when there's a war on, or hadn't you noticed?

Sgt Mumford Yes, ma'am, I had. We're the latest draft – just over from Ontario.

Louie Your first week here?

Sgt Mumford My first day.

Louie Oh. Then I shouldn't think anything will've arrived for you yet.

Sgt Mumford Don't you believe it – my girl back home, she wrote to me before I even left – just to make sure I'd have something to open when I got here.

Louie Well, if I can get past you to the receiving office, you'll be able to find out.

Sgt Mumford Hey, is this the big British welcome we were told to expect?

Louie It's the British postal system. Deliveries only to the office. You can pick it up from there.

Sgt Mumford All right, all right – you win Postie. I wouldn't want to foul up the system when I've only just arrived.

Louie And my name's not Postie.

Sgt Mumford No? What is it then?

Louie None of your business. Can I get through please?

Sgt Mumford Hey now, wait a minute.

Louie You are holding up His Majesty's post.

Sgt Mumford Well, ma'am, far be it from me to do any such thing.

Louie It's probably a serious criminal offence.

Sgt Mumford Holding up the post? It may well be – but tell me, do you have any more deliveries to make after this one?

Louie I'll say! You're just the first – there's a 20 mile round to do before I get back to the post office.

Sgt Mumford In that case I'd better help you.

Louie You can't do that! You're supposed to stay here in the camp.

Sgt Mumford That's not the sort of help I meant.

Louie Can I get past please!

Sgt Mumford Sure, but you won't get far.

Louie I don't know what you're talking about! Please let me …

Sgt Mumford I'm talking about your bicycle – it has a flat tyre!

Scene 3

In Liphook Post Office, later that morning

John Thompson is talking to eight year-old Joe Leggett

John Now then, young master Leggett, what have you come in for today, eh?

Joe Just a penny'th of gob-stoppers, please Mr Thompson.

John A penny'th of gob-stoppers? *(Starts to get the sweets out)* A penny'th of gob-stoppers. Do you know how much training it takes to be a postmaster these days, master Leggett?

Joe No, sir.

John No? Well I'll tell you. It takes many years of hard and dedicated work – several examinations to be passed, interviews to be attended, rules and regulations of His Majesty's postal service to be learnt by rote and thoroughly applied, staff to be managed, the latest telegraphic equipment to be installed and understood – and what do you come in here and ask me for? A penny'th of gob-stoppers!

Joe Sorry, Mr Thompson.

John Well that's how it is. We must all learn to do each other's work at a time of national crisis – if my shop assistant goes off doing a postman's round because the postman is fighting for King and Country in Flanders, then I must learn to be the shop assistant. *(He hands the sweets to Joe)* One penny, if you please.

Joe Thank you. *(Hands the penny over)*

John And thank you. Shall we be seeing you again tomorrow?

Joe I don't think so – my pocket money's all gone now.

John Then next week perhaps. Those should keep you going for a few days at least.

Joe Goodbye, Mr Thompson. *(He exits to the street)*

John Goodbye for now. *(Checking his pocket watch)* Now where's that wretched girl got to? She should have been back an hour ago.

Flora enters from the house

Flora No sign of Louie yet?

John Always late. Don't know what she does with her time out there.

Flora She's young.

John That's no excuse – she's taken on a responsible position – we must be able to rely on her. We're short-handed enough as it is.

Flora Yes, John.

John No good you "yes John"-ing me like that. You know I'm right.

Flora Yes, J.... Would you like me to start sorting the afternoon deliveries?

John I mean you – you're not even officially on the staff, yet you work harder than the rest of them put together.

Flora Well I have had a little more experience in post offices than some of them. The work comes naturally to me.

John Living next door to the job – never get away from it, that's the trouble. When this war's over we'll get a little cottage the other end of the village. Then you can be a housewife, not a post office clerk.

Flora I'm not sure which is worse.

John What's that?

Flora I'll get on with the sorting.

John She'll come in with some cock-and-bull story, you wait and see. Got another puncture, or some such.

Flora It's a very old bike she's riding. Bought it from Jess West for thirty shillings when she joined us.

John Every postman, or postwoman, has to provide their own conveyance for deliveries – you know the rules – and a *dependable* conveyance.

Flora I'll go and give Harry a hand.

John And no talking in the sorting office.

Flora I know – that's the rules too.

Flora starts to exit into the house,

but stops as Louie enters in haste through the shop door

Louie I'm sorry I'm late back – I had another …

John Miss Woods – what do you think you are doing?

Louie It was that bicycle again. It just …

John Where do you think you are?

Louie Why, what do you mean, Mr Thompson?

John Who do you think you are? Coming into the shop like this – like a member of the public.

Louie I'm sorry, Mr Thompson – but I was so late, and I saw you there as I passed by the window and I thought I'd …

John You are not paid to think, Miss Woods. You are paid to obey the rules as laid down by His Majesty's Post Office. You will go out again and enter the premises by the rear entrance as the regulations require.

Louie Yes, Mr Thompson. Sorry, Mr Thompson.

John And when you have done that, and reported yourself present to Mr Baker, I shall wish to see you in my office.

Louie Yes, Mr Thompson.

John That is all, Miss Woods.

Louie looks despairingly at Flora, then exits

(To Flora) And it's no good you giving her sympathetic looks whenever I have to discipline her.

Flora She's only nineteen, John. Were you any better at that age?

John If I wasn't, my mother would soon let me know it – and not just with the sharp edge of her tongue either.

Flora Times are changing, John.

John Yes, and not for the better I think. Now, you were going to help with the sorting, were you not?

Flora *(Sighing)* Yes, John.

Scene 4

Lynchmere Common

Bill & Maggie Tidy arrive home – he is a tinker and grinder

Bill *(Entering)* Now then, Mrs Tidy, you'd best leave the donkey out there. There be no room for 'un in here.

Maggie *(Off)* I do know that, Bill Tidy – I weren't born yesterday you know.

Bill Well there's times when I do wonder. Where's me 'baccy?

Maggie *(Entering)* Where he always is, I 'spect.

Bill searches his clothing and finds it – starts filling his pipe

Bill You making tea?

Maggie Soon as I gets the fire going. Don't be so fretful.

Bill I'm not being fretful.

Maggie Ever since the author'ties came round.

Bill They can't do a thing. I've no time to waste worrying about they.

Maggie Stop being fretful then.

Bill They wants to turn us out, but they'll find they can't do it.

Bill lights up his pipe

We've got squatters' rights. Squatters' rights – you know what that means?

Maggie You'se going to tell me – again.

Bill Nearly forty years we've been here. *(Waving his pipe)* The King of England hisself couldn't turn us out now.

Maggie It's not the King of England as is trying to do it.

Bill Nor lords of the manor neither. T'would take more than a lord of the manor to shift such as we.

Maggie You hopes.

Bill I knows. It's the law of the land. Your magistrates and lords of the manor can't go against the law of the land. It's in violet.

Maggie It's in what?

Bill In violet.

Maggie What's that mean?

Bill Don't you know anything? That's the colour they write laws in – in the law books. A sort of deep purple …

Maggie I knows what violet is. I just don't think you know what you're talking about sometimes. I'll go and make your tea.

Bill Donkey needs feeding.

Maggie So do I. The donkey can wait.

Bill He's had a hard pull today. Up to Hindhead and back.

Maggie If you got off and walked up the hills he wouldn't have to pull so hard. You and the grindstone.

Bill He'll be all right so long as he's fed. How much did us take today?

Maggie Before us stopped by at the last pub, you mean?

Bill A man needs his drink – grinding razors and scissors all day. And you were putting the gin away too.

Maggie I'm not going to sit outside in the cart a'waiting for you to come out, am I.

Bill Bit of drink does a wight no harm.

Maggie A bit of drink! The donkey stops by hisself every time he goes past a pub these days, to save you the trouble of doin' it.

Bill *(Going to exit)* I'll go and feed him if you're not.

Maggie Going to get rid of your beer more like. And take yerself well away from the doorpost a'fore you do it this time. *(To herself)* How much did us take! Some of us can't even hold what we do take.

Scene 5

In Flora's room, Liphook Post Office

Flora is consoling Louie

Flora Don't worry, Louie. I know you did your best.

Louie My bag was full. I'd only got to Conford. I'd another sixteen miles to go on my round – how could I have taken it?

Flora I sometimes think the people who make these regulations have never stepped foot outside London. Would you like a cup of coffee?

Louie *(Shyly)* Oh, no thank you – I don't …   *(Flora has not heard and carries on talking)*

Flora I remember once being carpeted for not delivering a telegram on time – we had a thunderstorm so violent it killed a cow in the next field, but that wasn't a good enough reason for the authorities. I had to write to them and say it would never happen again.

Louie I was very polite to the lady. I did try to explain I'd no room to take her parcel.

Flora I'm told she can be a difficult person at times. Here's your coffee.

Louie *(Accepting it with embarrassment)* Oh, thank you.

Flora You'll find Mr Thompson's love for the post office sometimes makes him apply the rules a little strictly. And as he had received an official complaint from the lady he felt he had to pass it on.

Louie *(Nods)*

Flora And he made you sign an apology.

Louie Yes.

Flora Well, that's an end to it then. Mr Thompson's not a man to bear grudges.

Louie I hope not.

Flora *(Changing the subject)* You've not been in my little room here before, have you?

Louie No. It's very – cosy.

Flora *(Laughs)* I'm not sure cosy is quite the word I'd use. A writing desk, two chairs, a waste paper basket and a potted plant. It's where I try to write – away from the family.

Louie Do you write a lot?

Flora Not as much as I'd like to. What with the children to look after and the post office work to do. I'll show you a few of my scraps.

Flora goes to pick up some papers from the side. Louie has been nervously nursing her unwanted coffee, and takes this opportunity to pour it into the pot plant.

These are some little poems – nothing very sophisticated, I'm afraid. Take a look and tell me what you think.

She notices Louie's empty cup.

Oh, you drank that quickly – would you like some more coffee?

Louie No! No, thank you. One's quite enough.

Flora *(Indicating the poems)* They're no great works of literature.

Louie I think it's very clever, writing anything like this. Oh look – there's one called 'Heather'.

Flora The purple moorland. It's the thing that first struck me about this area. So different from the cornfields where I grew up.

Louie It starts, *(she reads)* 'You talk of pale primroses, of frail and fragrant posies …' I love primroses, don't you? – it means spring's really here when they come out.

Flora You notice things like that much more when you're out on the early rounds, don't you think? I miss it now, doing the sorting in the office.

Louie *(Reads on)* 'The cowslip and the cuckoo-flower that scent the spring-time lea. But give to me the heather, the honey-scented heather, the glowing gypsy heather – that's the flower for me!' Do you really prefer it here to where you were born?

Flora I sometimes miss all the old sights and smells I grew up with. Skylarks rising out of the fields right by my window, large flat fields stretching away to a distant line of trees, corn and oats sighing and rustling in the breeze, heavy earthy scents, not sharp like here …. One day perhaps I'll try to write about those times too. At the moment it's just what I see and feel here in Hampshire.

Louie We're not such a bad lot.

Flora There I go again – I was thinking of places and you're bringing it back to people.

Louie Well yes – it's people that make places, isn't it?

Flora You're right. There was old Queenie with her bees and her lace making, for instance. I could write a fine story about her.

Louie And your family.

Flora Yes. Though I'm not sure I'd be very comfortable writing things that people could identify as being about themselves.

Louie You mean there were scandals?

Flora Not really – nothing compared to what I've seen and heard since. It's just *(shrugs)* I don't know – I'd be uncomfortable, that's all.

Louie Then give everybody false names, like they do in novels. 'To protect the innocent'.

Flora *(Laughing)* Louie Woods – I might just do that!

Louie I wish I could write.

Flora Anyone can write, if they want to.

Louie But how can you just shut yourself away in here and do it? Doesn't Mr Thompson mind?

Flora Oh, he thinks of it as a harmless distraction – a strange whim which his wife has – like my bringing wild flowers into the house and putting them in a vase on the supper table.

Louie *(Unsure)* I see.

Flora Mind you, he has his fishing. And how anyone can find pleasure in dragging a happy living thing from its cool, clear home with a hook has always been beyond me.

Louie Lots of us fish the ponds round here – seems natural. You should see the pike they get out sometimes. Big enough to feed a whole family for days.

Flora The most Mr Thompson seems to come back with is a couple of medium sized perch or tench. Anyway, you'd better be off now or you'll be in more trouble – and that would never do.

Louie No. Thank you for listening – it's made me feel a lot better.

Flora That's all right. I do know how it feels. Now be careful on your way home, won't you – and mind the soldiers.

Louie Don't worry, I will. See you tomorrow morning. *(Exits)*

Flora *(After her)* Bright and early. *(A pause, then to herself)* I <u>do</u> know how it feels. Now then, Flora – you're getting maudlin again, and that will never do.

Scene 6

On the road from Forest Mere

John Thompson and Harry Envis are walking back after a day's fishing

Harry Not a bad day's fishing, Mr Thompson.

John Not for you, Harry. Did you know that pike was in there?

Harry Oh, I've been after 'un for a while. But I reckon he's only a tiddler compared with some that's there. Not been cleaned out for some time, that pool. They grows to over twenty pound down there when they're not disturbed. Mind you, not much good for eating that size.

John What's that one then?

Harry 'Bit over two foot – seven pounds or so I should say – just right. We'll soak him in salt water twelve hours to get the mud out of him, then steam him and serve him with parsley sauce – he'll make a good dish.

John Enough for several of you there.

Harry Nearly got a second one too, but I couldn't strike at the right angle – hook slid out of his bony mouth. What did you get?

John Just a pair of medium sized perch. About a pound and a half each, I should think. They'll be nice split open and grilled.

Harry They will too. Mrs Thompson enjoys cooking, does she?

John She's a good cook.

Harry Oh ar.

John Her family always cooked for themselves. She learned from her mother.

Harry Difficult times these. A nice piece of fish'll make a change from the usual stodge.

John What else did you catch, besides the pike?

Harry Couple of perch worth keeping – like you. Arrived too late to get tench.

John Always fish the same swim, do you?

Harry Bait it up a few days in advance if I can – did you see my rabbit on the stick?

John Is that what it was?

Harry Old rabbit carcass crawling with maggots. Hang it over the water and let them drop in for a day or two. Brings the fish like nothing else. Trouble was that old pike kept everything else away today.

John You made him pay for it in the end.

Harry Wasn't sure I'd got a heavy enough line on him. Lucky he didn't get in among the roots or he'd have got clean away.

John What were you using on the hook?

Harry Red worms mostly, for the perch. Tried a bit of bread paste earlier, but it didn't seem to bring anything along. You never can tell. Today was a red worm day. How about you?

John Lobworm.

Harry Well, it caught you two for the kitchen. Can't complain I suppose.

John Might have hoped for a few more, or bigger.

Harry They're always there for another day, that's what I say. And there's nothing quite as peaceful as another day's fishing.

John That's true. When duty permits.

Harry Oh aye, Mr Thompson, oh aye – when duty permits.

Scene 7

In the Postmaster's House, soon after

Flora enters, talking to Diana who is off-stage

Flora Homework, Di! – if it's not done by the time you go to school tomorrow, it's you who'll have to explain to your schoolteacher, not me or your father. I'm going to try and get some writing done myself while the house is quiet – so you can do the same.

There is a knock at the front door

Lawk 'a' mussy-O, now who can that be at the door? *(Moving to answer it)* Folk always come when I'm about to start something. If it's one of your friends, Di, I'll tell them you're busy and … *(She is now at the door and opens it – and is visibly surprised at who she finds there)* Oh! Dr Macfie.

Macfie Found you, in your new abode at last.

Flora You're the last person I expected see.

Macfie A pleasant surprise, I hope.

Flora Of course, as always. Won't you come in?

Macfie Thank you. I must say your streets are busier than I expected. Almost had to fight my way from the station.

Flora There are two camps here both sending men to the front today.

Macfie Poor devils. Straight from the prairies to the slaughterhouse. But what a topic of conversation to begin with – and when I have not seen you for so long. How are the children?

Flora Diana is in the other room, pretending to do her homework.

Macfie Still insisting she is not really called Winifred, I see.

Flora We're used to it now. She'll be 13 soon, and knows her own mind, that one.

Macfie And young Basil?

Flora He'll be seven in October. He's out with friends at the moment – I was just going to take advantage of the peace and quiet to do a little work.

Macfie And then I arrived – I am sorry!

Flora You are very welcome, as always. Can I get you some coffee? I have a pot freshly made.

They move into Flora's room

Macfie A cup of coffee would be much appreciated. So this is your writers nest?

Flora It serves as one.

Macfie Complete with potted plant, I see.

Flora *(Getting coffee)* Yes – but not in the best of health at the moment. Perhaps I've been overwatering it.

Macfie And this is where the world yields you the right to earn your scanty leisure.

Flora In return for the precious opportunity known as Life.

Macfie I remember you saying that in Bournemouth, the last time I visited you.

Flora I do feel a little guilty when my pen is idle.

Macfie We are all trying to produce something from within ourselves which will be immortal. Unrecognised perhaps, but nonetheless immortal. Wasn't Shakespeare alluding to that in his sonnet?

Flora "So long as men can breathe, or eyes can see, So long lives this, and this gives life to thee."

Macfie That's the one.

Flora But what with the long hours in the post office, and then the cooking and housework to do …

Macfie You appreciate why I renounced any idea of a domestic life myself. I am free to take a few months here and a few months there to write out all the poetry and philosophy in me.

Flora I don't think that will ever be my destiny. By the end of the year I shall be forty …

Macfie Forty, what is forty? I am nearly fifty – but if I could have just ten years left to write I should be content. Look forward! Look for the opportunity – it will come.

Flora I have written a few pieces – but nothing like your published odes.

Macfie Nor should they be. We must each go our own path. Classical odes are not your style.

Flora No. But then I'm not sure what is. I feel such gifts as I have are for poetry.

Macfie Well that may be so. You must let me see a collection of your work some time – perhaps I could help you find a publisher.

Flora 'Flora Thompson, the postmistress poet!' I think that unlikely somehow.

Macfie If you aim at nothing, you will surely hit nothing.

Flora That's true.

Macfie As true as I sit here.

Flora Perhaps, when my commitments are fewer …

Macfie But you must make your writing a commitment.

Flora I get up before daybreak as it is!

Macfie Aye. I'm not saying it's easy.

Flora After this abysmal war is over let's hope we shall all have a little more freedom to do as we wish.

Macfie It can't go on for much longer. And the children are less of a tie than they were a few years back.

Flora That's starting to be true. Diana can be almost helpful at times.

Macfie And young Basil is not quite the handful he was, I'll be bound.

Flora I can see you've never had a family. He's a younger version of his father, and just as stubborn.

Macfie I see. And Mr Thompson is as implacable towards your writing as ever.

Flora John? He's not likely to change. Not unless I make some money from it – then perhaps he might begin to think it worthwhile.

Macfie Then let me help.

Flora Dear Ronald …

Macfie I remember your parable to me about that parasite, the dodder – how it drags the heather down to the ground on the heaths around here. You told me – or rather, you implied – that while you were a heather person, your husband was like the dodder.

Flora Did I say that? It was just an idea I had for a novel. I don't suppose it will ever get written.

Macfie I think it was more than that.

Flora You should not read too much into a plot for a story. I'm sure that …

Macfie We must somehow lift the dodder from you, and let you breathe again.

John Thompson has arrived back from his fishing

John *(Off)* Flora!

Flora I'm sure that won't be necessary. I am breathing quite healthily at the moment. *(Calling to John)* In here, John.

Macfie He is master of your house, but not of your talents.

John Thompson enters, back from his fishing

John Ah, Dr Macfie. Given us the benefit of one of your chance visits again I see.

Macfie I was in the area, Mr Thompson, just passing through.

John Good. You found us then.

Flora How was the fishing?

John Harry had more luck than I did. There's two perch in the kitchen though – better than nothing.

Macfie That's when the bravado of the fisherman's yarn meets the reality of the housewife's pan.

John Yes.

Flora I'll cook them for us tonight.

John Are you not staying for a meal, Dr Macfie?

Macfie No, no – I am a bird of passage, thank you Mr Thompson. Expected in London tonight.

John But doubtless we shall see you again.

Macfie When my itinerary permits. It is always a pleasure to talk for a while with a fellow lover of literature.

John The London trains leave at half past the hour, I believe. Now if you will excuse me, I am told I have to help our daughter on a point of mathematics. *(Exits)*

Macfie I didn't embarrass you I hope.

Flora The dodder cannot help being dodder – it was made that way.

Macfie Aye. *(Pause)* I think I should take the next train. Lord knows how long it will take to get to London tonight with all these troop movements going on. Shall I be welcome to call again?

Flora I have said, you are always welcome.

Macfie And you will send me some of your poetry to read.

Flora Now you do embarrass me!

Macfie Genius, my dear Mrs Thompson, very rarely recognises itself. And now I must leave you to cook your fresh perch, an occupation for which, unlike you, I'm sure I have absolutely no talent.

Flora There's a world of a difference though, my dear Dr Ronald Macfie, between talent and genius.

Scene 8

On the Road with Maggie Tidy

Maggie is calling for business

Maggie Any old razors or scissors to grind, Mr Tidy he's comin' be'ind!

Joe Leggett enters

Any old razors or scissors to grind, Mr Tidy he's comin' be'ind!

Joe I've got this old penknife needs sharpening.

Maggie Razors, scissors, scythes, and shears; billhooks and blades, swords and spears. Mr Tidy grinds 'em all, be they big or be they small.

Joe All I've got is this old knife.

Maggie Let's 'ave a look at 'ee then.

Joe hands her his knife

What's this? A winkle-picker?

Joe It's a good one – I got it for my birthday.

Maggie *(Holding it up)* Lor'. One good grind on Mr Tidy's wheel and it'd be gone.

Joe It's a bit blunt.

Maggie Blunt is it? So it is. Well, you'll just have to trust Mr Tidy to do a special gentle job on this. One slip and *(she sucks her teeth)*. 'Ave you never seen Mr Tidy working at 'is grinding wheel?

Joe Can't say I have.

Maggie You should see the sparks fly when he gets up a good speed on it. But he does do a good job. All the reg'lars says so. You take 'un along to 'im.

Maggie indicates off-stage, and Joe exits

Sgt Mumford enters from the opposite direction

Sgt Mumford Say, are you the wife of this Bill Tidy our Postie's been telling us about?

Maggie Depends on what your Postie's been saying.

Sgt Mumford Oh, she's been saying that this Bill Tidy is the best knife grinder in the country. Puts an edge on a razor blade sharp enough to split a hair lengthways, she says.

Maggie She does? Well that's my Bill all right. Got an eye like an 'awk and an 'and as steady as the Buffs.

Sgt Mumford And she also said that you and Mr Tidy know more about the countryside round here than anyone else she could think of.

Maggie That's right. He can tell you about every bird, bush, tree and flower on the common, without a word of a lie. Knows when anything's goin' on that shouldn't be too – acts like he owns the place sometimes.

Sgt Mumford Well, I'm mighty proud to make your acquaintance.

Maggie Tell that to the magistrates then, that keep trying to move us off our land.

Sgt Mumford Move you? I thought you were part of the furnishings here.

Maggie Don't know about words like that. You're one of them Americans aren't you? Don't know about words like that.

Sgt Mumford I mean you've always been here.

Maggie Since Adam delved an' Eve span, as Mr Tidy 'ud say.

Sgt Mumford That's near enough always, I guess.

Maggie Oh, we can tell you a story or two about this place, Mr Tidy and me, I can tell you.

Sgt Mumford I'll bet you can.

Maggie That chestnut tree in the village, f'r instance.

Sgt Mumford The one in the square, opposite the blacksmith's?

Maggie Aye. That's the famous one, y'know. In that song.

Sgt Mumford What, 'Under the spreading chestnut tree the village smithy stands'? That one?

Maggie That's 'im. That's 'im.

Sgt Mumford You don't say! Now that's really something. Wait till I tell the lads back at the camp.

Maggie Aye, you tell 'em. There's 'istory 'ere goes back a long way – further 'n where you comes from, I'll be bound.

Sgt Mumford Well, I don't rightly know …

Maggie And rights too. We've got rights.

Sgt Mumford Oh yeah, I remember at school – the Magna Carta.

Maggie Carters, and knife grinders too. We've all got rights. Them's with money thinks different, but they'd better watch out.

Sgt Mumford Uh-huh.

Maggie You got anything for grindin'?

Sgt Mumford Er, not at this moment, ma'am. But I'll be sure to tell the camp barber. The way he draws blood right now, he could do with a good honing.

Maggie Could 'ee? Pity – we only does grindin'.

Scene 9

In Liphook Post Office, summer 1917

Flora is just finishing the early morning sorting at 5.45am
when Louie enters

Louie Morning Mrs Thompson.

Flora Good morning, Louie. On time as usual.

Louie Quarter to six on the dot. I'm all right in the summer, even with this new Summer Time idea – it's the winters I find difficult.

Flora Don't I know it.

Louie At least you can see where you're going at this time of year.

Flora By the time you start, you can. Your round's stacked over there. And there was a letter for you – I've put it on top of the pile.

Louie Oh, let's see. I wonder who it's from?

Flora One of your soldier friends, I should think.

Louie Yes, but which one?

Flora *(Teasing)* Louie Woods, you're not two-timing those poor lads in the camp, are you?

Louie Nothing serious. They call me 'Postie'. It's all good-natured.

Flora Well don't open it now. 'Postie' had better pick up her bag and get ready for her round before Mr Thompson comes in – he won't be so good-natured if he finds her reading her private correspondence here.

Louie No. Hope the bicycle doesn't give up on me today.

Flora So do I. And no stopping for tea too long at Woodman's Green either.

Louie Oh, she's a lovely lady there. She invites me in the house to sit down, but I have to stay outside because of the rules.

Flora Quite right.

Louie And keep the post bag on my back.

Flora At all times.

Louie I think the rules were made thinking all postmen were Olympic athletes.

Flora Well I'm afraid Mr Thompson's not one to relax them. Listen, I think I hear him coming. Ready for inspection now?

Louie Just about.

Flora *(Checking)* Shoes and buttons polished? Jacket pressed? Boater straight? Badge on left lapel? Yes, you'll probably pass.

Louie I hope so.

John enters

John Right, Miss Woods. Ready for your round? Good, good. *(Starts to inspect her)* Let's see. Strand of hair loose there. And the badge could do with a bit more of a polish tomorrow. Yes. Other than that … Got your bag? Good. Yes, that all seems satisfactory. Off you go then.

Louie exits

(After her) And don't be late back.

Flora And I must be off too, through to the house to get your breakfast and the children ready for school.

John All the deliveries sorted then?

Flora They are. We're clear to receive collections now.

John Right. And what are we eating this morning? Not stewed snails again I hope.

Flora I think not. I'd rather have no meat at all than try that again.

John Tasted like old rubber.

Flora I think the French must use a different variety. I'm afraid it's just bread and cheese this morning. And I even had to queue to get that, yesterday.

John No pickle?

Flora There's a bit of home-made pickle left. And I'll make you some tea.

John Good.

Flora And after that, if I can be spared, I should very much like to take a walk.

John You'll be back to sort the second delivery this afternoon?

Flora Of course.

John Very well then. Which direction will you be going in?

Flora I've a mind to revisit Grayshott. Strange how this promotion of yours should bring us back to within three miles of my old haunts.

John You'll take care going past the army camp.

Flora Yes. It's sad to think – in those days I was posting bulletins in the window to give news of a different war. We thought that one was terrible at the time, but now …

John Flanders has all but wiped out the memory of Mafeking and the rest.

Flora And Edwin, poor Edwin …

John A walk will do you good. But don't be late back.

Flora John, I am not Louie. I am your wife.

John And I am responsible for running this office, serving two busy army camps and a regular civilian population, short-handed. You know I push myself as hard as anyone else here.

Flora Yes John.

John And don't …

Flora I've no complaint. You are as fair as you are strict. Everyone says so.

John Yes, well –

Flora And now I shall go and perform miracles with a lump of hard cheddar and a cottage loaf.

John And pickles.

Flora And pickles, and a pot of tea. *(Exits)*

John When will this wretched war end?

Scene 10

On Bramshott Common, later that day

A British corporal is training Canadian troops

Corporal Come on, look lively. Don't just stan' there – git fell in! You don't fink Fritz is goin' to let yer spend all day sortin' yerselves out do yer? 'E'd have mown down the lot of yer by now. 'Ere you – wassyer name?

94

1st Canadian Soldier Pardon me?

Corporal You'll pardon me before I've finished with yer. I said wassyer name?

1st Canadian Soldier *What* sort of name?

Corporal Wassyer name – yer bleedin' moniker. You 'ave bin given one 'aven't yer? They don't leave you in the middle of the bleedin' prairies to find yer own, do they?

2nd Canadian Soldier *(To first)* I think he wants to know your name, Jim.

Corporal Well done that man! Full marks fer understanding the King's bleedin' English.

1st Canadian Soldier Signaller Johnson. Sir.

Corporal Nah then, nah then, no need to overdo it. Corporal will do. Well then signaller Johnson, now we know 'oo you are, p'raps you'd like to tell us what it was we was practisin' doin' 'ere yesterday afternoon.

1st Canadian Soldier Use of the bayonet, I guess.

Corporal You guess? You'd better do a bleedin' sight better than guess when yer out there in Flanders, my son, or it'll be goodbye Johnson in bleedin' short order. This is a war you're goin' to, not a bleedin' invitation to dance. Do I make myself clear?

1st Canadian Soldier Perfectly clear, corporal.

Corporal Oh good. Well just don't yer forget it, any of yer. Now what was it I said you 'ave to fink when yer lunging at Fritz wiv yer bayonet?

2nd Canadian Soldier *(Trying on the accent)* Fink 'ee's yer muvver-in-law!

Laughter from all the Canadians

Corporal Oh we've a bleedin' linguist 'ere, 'aven't we. Well as it 'appens you're right fer once. And fer those of you 'oo 'aven't got muvver-in-laws, yer can fink 'ee's the sergeant-major instead. *(More laughter)* Now then, for today's training. Johnson – what do yer fink I'm 'olding 'ere in my 'and?

1st Canadian Soldier Looks like an old tin filled with nuts and bolts to me, corporal.

Corporal Does it indeed? Well let me tell you, this 'ere tin represents a Mills bomb. You know what a Mills bomb is?

2nd Canadian Soldier You throw it. At the enemy.

Corporal You do, soldier – and as far away from you and yours as possible – because when it hits the ground, wallop! It is not a pretty sight if you're standin' too close.

95

2nd Canadian Soldier I'll bet.

Corporal And due to its tendency to cause mayhem and destruction, we are not going to practice wiv the real thing, but wiv this – which Signaller Johnson rightly identifies as an old jam tin filled wiv nuts and bolts …

2nd Canadian Soldier Well done, Jim.

1st Canadian Soldier Comes from a wasted childhood, Len.

Corporal Which, as luck would 'ave it, is the approximate size and weight of the aforementioned Mills bomb. Any questions?–No?–Good. Right, now over there we 'ave Fritz dug into them foxholes – see 'em? – nah, not there – there! – and on the command, you will bowl your Mills bomb from 'ere into one of them 'oles. Is that crystal?

2nd Canadian Soldier Er, *bowl* corporal? How's that again?

1st Canadian Soldier Sort of – throw it, you mean?

Corporal Gordon Bennett, 'ave I got to teach you colonials the rules of cricket too?

2nd Canadian Soldier I can sure pitch a good baseball.

1st Canadian Soldier Hit a fly on a wall at thirty yards.

Corporal Yer Fritz ain't no fly on the wall though, is 'ee – 'ee's a bleedin' Bosche buried in a bleedin' trench. You 'as ter lob yer grenade in an arc, so as it comes at 'im from above, see?

2nd Canadian Soldier I guess we don't play too much cricket in Manitoba.

Corporal Well it looks like I'm going ter 'ave to show you then, ain't I. Right, so over there is yer Bosche in a hole. *(They look where he points, somewhere conveniently off-stage.)* Now I takes my Mills bomb just so in my right 'and – pulls out the pin wiv me left 'and – and wiv an easy action, bowls it so it lands right on 'is middle stump – bang!

> *The Corporal demonstrates his bowling technique, using the filled tin*

So – which of yer's going to 'ave a go first?

1st Canadian Soldier Say, that looked pretty easy.

Corporal All right then, demon bowler – let's be 'aving yer.

> *He gives him a tin, and the soldier attempts to bowl – with less success*

Corporal Fritz'll die bleedin' laughing before you get 'im, soldier.
(To the 2nd soldier) Let's see if you can do any better …

The bowling lesson can continue for as long as the director of the play wishes, depending on cast, venue and audience. At the end, Flora appears from the general direction in which the 'bombs' are being thrown.

Corporal 'Old fire!

2nd Canadian Soldier You didn't tell us Fritz was female, corporal.

Corporal Very funny. *(To Flora)* Oy, you! You're on a firing range.

Flora Oh, I'm sorry.

1st Canadian Soldier It's all right, ma'am, we're only throwing jam tins today.

2nd Canadian Soldier Tomorrow it's the real thing.

Corporal Orl right, orl right. I'll get the tins back so yer can 'ave anuvver go – and in the meantime you two, escort this lady orf the range double quick. *(He walks off)*

1st Canadian Soldier Say, aren't you the village postmistress? Bit off your route today.

Flora I was walking home from the ponds – must have been daydreaming.

2nd Canadian Soldier Real nice countryside round here – I was writing home to the folks about it just the other day.

Flora Where's home?

2nd Canadian Soldier Near Winnipeg.

1st Canadian Soldier D'you know Canada?

Flora No, I don't. But my brother was there for a while.

1st Canadian Soldier He was? Whereabouts.

Flora In Ontario. Until the war started.

2nd Canadian Soldier He's over here now, then?

Flora *(Quietly)* He was.

2nd Canadian Soldier You mean … I'm sorry.

Flora That's what I was daydreaming about. I'd just been to the place where I was working when he was away in the Boer war. He came back from that one.

1st Canadian Soldier Say, when we get over there we'll give Fritz one for your brother.

Flora I hope the whole thing's over before you have to.

> *By this time they have moved away from the training area*

2nd Canadian Soldier Well I guess you can find your way home from here, ma'am. We'd better be getting back to our tin cans.

Flora Thank you. And I'm sorry I stopped your training.

1st Canadian Soldier The corporal may think differently, but for us it's sure been a privilege to meet you.

2nd Canadian Soldier And remember us to 'Postie'.

Flora I shall.

The soldiers exit

And to Edwin.

"For very deep my Love must sleep,
On that far Flemish plain,
If he does not know that the heath-bells blow
On the Hampshire hills again!"

A Gypsy woman enters

Gypsy woman Good day to you, miss.

Flora Oh – hello. You startled me.

Gypsy woman I could see that – you were in a world of your own.

Flora It's a lovely day.

Gypsy woman 'Tis for those as are up and about in it.

Flora Yes.

Gypsy woman My poor granddaughter's not though – she's out of sorts, and I'm looking for some wood-sage.

Flora Wood-sage?

Gypsy woman Good stiff dose of wood-sage tea'll soon set her right, see if it won't. Thought I remembered some growing in a clearing the other side of the ponds.

Flora Oh, there's a patch very much closer than that – just down there in fact – by the edge of those trees.

Gypsy woman You know your plants then, young lady.

Flora Not all of them, I'm afraid – but I try to look out for those I don't know, and read up about them when I get home.

Gypsy woman Not many people take an interest these days, that's the trouble. All the old knowledge – it'll die when the likes of me are gone.

Flora I hope not.

Gypsy woman You mark my words. All these doctors and their 'ospitals – be the death of it all. Death of <u>us</u> too, probably. Never get me into an 'ospital, never.

Flora You certainly don't look in need of …

Gypsy woman Eighty-nine, me. There – would you believe that? Eighty-nine and all me own teeth. And I'll tell you what, there's not many my age these days as can say that.

Flora I'm sure you're right …

Gypsy woman It's the food they eat today, you know – it's not natural. Not natural at all.

Flora No, I suppose not …

Gypsy woman You've got children, haven't you.

Flora Why yes, I've got two. How did you know …

Gypsy woman Yes, I can see it in your face. It's all writ in the face, what a person is. And if you know what a person is, you can tell pretty well how things'll go with them in the future.

Flora You're a fortune teller?

Gypsy woman I believe in trading favour for favour. You've shown me where the wood-sage grows – I can tell you that you're goin' to be loved.

Flora But I have a husband!

Gypsy woman Loved by a lot o' folk – by people all over.

Flora What do you mean?

Gypsy woman Strangers will become your friends.

Flora Strangers?

Gypsy woman Aye – strangers who'll never even meet you will know you and love you.

Flora But how?

Gypsy woman That's for you to work out, my dear. But there's some good news coming your way, that I can tell you. Now I must go and pick my herbs. *(Exits)*

Flora And I must be getting back too, or I'll be late for the afternoon delivery – and then where should we be?

Scene 11

Liphook Post Office, soon after

Harry Envis and Louie enter

Louie What was that the landlord said?

Harry Nothing I'd want to repeat in your tender ears, my dear.

Louie Oh, that's not fair. I'm in the 'Dragon' with you all every lunchtime – it's not as if I don't get to hear bad language.

Harry Who said it was bad language?

Louie Why was he whispering then?

Harry *(Teasing)* There's reasons for whispering other than bad language, you know.

Louie Harry Envis, are you going to tell me or not.

Harry That depends.

Louie On what.

Harry On whether I can trust you to keep a secret.

Louie Course I can. What was it?

Harry I don't know though. If I tell you, it'll likely be all over 'Tin Town' by first post tomorrow.

Louie Postgirl's honour.

Harry Is there honour among postgirls?

Louie You're not going to tell me, are you.

Harry Impatient, that's the trouble with you young girls today. I'm getting to it.

Louie Well let me know when you arrive.

Harry Hang on, that's Mr Thompson arriving. Look busy!

Harry hangs up his coat and Louie finds some letters to sort.
John Thompson enters.

John No sign of Mrs Thompson?

Harry Not yet, Mr Thompson – but the main delivery hasn't come yet.

John I was expecting her back before this. Miss Woods, I hope you will tidy your hair again before you start your round.

Louie Yes, Mr Thompson.

John I'm not sure that I altogether approve of you spending your time in the 'Green Dragon'.

Harry We look after her, Mr Thompson.

John I'm glad to hear it, Harry. *(To Louie)* I assume your parents are aware that you take your lunchtimes in a public house.

Louie Yes, they are, Mr Thompson.

John Well, times have changed since I was a lad on the Isle of Wight. *(He exits)*

Louie We look after her!

Harry Well we do, don't we?

Louie Makes it sound like the east end of London, not a Hampshire village. And the pub's only next door.

Harry He told me once his parents were very strict with him.

Louie What's he like when you go fishing?

Harry We get on fine. He's quite a different character off-duty.

Louie Well I suppose Mrs Thompson must find something in him.

Harry Not too loud – he might hear you!

Louie Sometimes I think he leaves his office door open just so that he can listen to us.

Harry Better be careful what you say then.

Louie Look, there's a letter still here for Mrs Thompson – came in this morning's delivery. *(She examines it)*

Harry Here, you'll be trying to read it through the envelope next. Put it to one side.

Louie From London. From that Dr Macfie, I'd say.

Harry You're supposed to sort the post, not vet it.

Louie She sent him some of her poems to read. I wonder if this is him saying what he thinks of them.

Harry *(Again)* Put it to one side.

Louie She wants to be a writer.

Harry She is a writer.

Louie She's written a few short stories, she told me. Had them published in magazines.

Harry That's being a writer.

Louie Not a proper writer – at least she doesn't think so.

Harry It's more of one than I'll ever be.

Louie I wouldn't have the patience.

Harry I said you were impatient.

Louie Oh yes, and what was it you were trying not to tell me just now.

Harry Not that again.

Louie Yes that again.

Harry It's really nothing important.

Louie In that case it doesn't matter if I know.

Harry All he said was …

Louie Well?

Harry He'd heard Mrs Vale say the postmaster's house always smelt of lino and bacon.

Louie Is that all … ?

At this moment Flora enters quickly

Flora Sorry I'm a bit late. Has anything arrived yet?

Louie No, we're still waiting for it to cook – er, come.

Flora I wonder where it's got to?

Harry Probably shunted into a lino – I mean a siding.

Flora That won't make Mr Thompson any happier.

Harry He was just asking after you.

Flora Yes, thank you, I saw him as I came in.

Louie And there's a letter came for you this morning.

Flora *(Taking it)* For me? I wonder who…? No, I'd best open it later.

Harry If you don't mind me saying so, Mrs Thompson, you're looking a bit rushed off your feet today

Flora No more than the rest of us, Harry.

Louie You could read your letter while we're waiting. We'll keep a look-out.

Flora For the post?

Harry I think she meant for Mr Thompson!

Flora *(Laughing, opening the letter)* This is not a good example for the postmaster's wife to be setting. *(A pause while she reads)*

Harry Good news?

Flora The gypsy was right.

Louie Gypsy?

Flora Dr Macfie has found a publisher for my poetry.

Louie *(To Harry)* See? *(Harry makes a rude gesture back at her)*

Flora 'So we may now hope to see your collection of verses in print.'

Harry A famous author in the village.

Flora A small collection of verses published hardly makes me famous, Harry.

Harry It's a start though. Even the most famous had to start somewhere.

Louie Post's arriving! *(She exits)*

Flora *(To Harry)* So they did.

Harry Aye. Well, we'd better get back to work. *(Turning back as he goes)* You coming through to the sorting office, Mrs Thompson? *(He exits)*

Flora Yes, Harry, I'm coming. We mustn't let poetry get in the way of the post.

Macfie enters

Macfie You received my letter I see.

Flora Ronald! But …

Macfie The postmistress poet.

Flora So soon. I didn't expect …

Macfie I was passing. Is the time …?

Flora Inconvenient? A little, yes.

Macfie Then I shall not stay.

Flora I should like to have the time to thank you properly.

Macfie But poetry must not get in the way of the post – I heard you say it.

Flora That was ungrateful of me, after all you've done.

Macfie It was not meant for my ears. And you are right – I also have work which must be attended to.

John *(Off)* Flora, are you there?

Macfie And I see you have too.

Flora I'm sorry.

> *John Thompson enters – he does not notice Macfie*

John <u>There</u> you are. The afternoon post …

Flora … will be delayed if I don't come and help. I know. I'm coming.

John Sometimes I think we live in different worlds, Flora, you and I. *(He exits)*

Flora If the world is in your imagination, then you may be right.

Macfie Imagination – aye, maybe it's all in the imagination. *(He exits, unseen by her)*

Flora I must go – you understand … *(She sees Macfie has gone)* Dear Ronald.

Scene 12

On the Road with Bill & Maggie Tidy

Maggie is calling for business again

Maggie Any old razors or scissors to grind, Mr Tidy he's comin' be'ind!

(To audience) 'Ere, sir, you're not short of a few pence, are you? Only it's my Bill's birthday today and I've nothing for 'im. First time it's ever 'appened. Enough to buy 'im a screw of 'baccy for 'is birthday, 'ave you? You're a gentleman, sir. He's not 'imself without 'is 'baccy.

Madam, what lovely flowers you 'ave in your garden there. It's my man's birthday, you know, and 'ee do love flowers so. 'Ee'd be so pleased if I could take 'im just a few. No, those just there. You're very kind. Dahlias are they? My, what a lovely bunch – 'ee will love those.

Any old razors or scissors to grind, Mr Tidy he's comin' be'ind!

Bill *(Entering)* Where 'ave you got to, you old faggot.

Maggie Don't you 'old faggot' me, Bill Tidy. While you'se been kippin' in the undergrowth back there, I'se been a-carryin' on doin' business.

Bill Oh? And what sort o' business be that, then?

Maggie *(Shows him the flowers)* Look, what d'you think to them?

Bill For me?

Maggie For you? Lor, give me strength!

Bill Only, I likes flowers.

Maggie I knows you likes flowers. I told the lady you likes flowers.

Bill And it's me birthday – you remembered!

Maggie I did, but they're not for you.

Bill But I likes 'em.

Maggie You likes your beer too, and more than we can afford – that's your trouble. These are for 'er across the road.

Bill Who's that then?

Maggie You'll see. *(She mimes knocking at a door)* Good day ma'am – fresh flowers, straight from the garden. Set your rooms off a treat, they will. Only thruppence a bunch. You're very kind ma'am. Thank you.

She sells the flowers to a stooge

Bill How much is that you've got?

Maggie Never you mind. This 'ere money's mine. 'Bout all I do 'ave.

Bill And on me birthday. Nothing for me?

Maggie Depends.

Bill What on?

Maggie You.

Bill Me what?

Maggie You bein' a gentleman to me.

Bill What's one of them?

Maggie If you don't know by now, Bill Tidy, I'm not telling you.

Bill We got enough for a drink? On me birthday?

Maggie No thanks to you if we 'ave.

Bill Only comes round once a year, me birthday.

Maggie More's the pity – I'd be rid of you quicker if it came oftner.

Bill All right then, you old faggot, you can make yer own way home.

Maggie But I have got yer a screw of 'baccy.

Bill 'Baccy. And I thought you'd forgot.

Maggie Couldn't forget you if I tried, Mr Tidy, and that's the truth.

Scene 13

Flora's room, Liphook Post Office, early 1918

Flora is sitting writing – Louie enters

Louie Sorry to disturb you, Mrs Thompson.

Flora Oh – hello Louie. What is it.

Louie I know you don't like being interrupted on your time off …

Flora It's all right – I can't seem to put two thoughts together today anyway.

Louie You look a bit – pale. Are you feeling all right?

Flora Yes, Louie, I'm fine thank you. We had some unexpected news yesterday, Mr Thompson and I, that's all.

Louie Only there's a lady and her daughter in the shop asking to see you.

Flora For me?

Louie She's talking to Mr Thompson. He said I'd better come and get you because you don't like him coming in here.

Flora *(Laughs)* He's afraid he wouldn't understand the things I write about.

Louie Wouldn't he?

Flora Just my little joke, Louie – of course he would. Mr Thompson's been properly educated – not dragged up in the back of beyond like I was.

Louie *(Unsure how to take this)* Oh.

Flora Who is this lady?

Louie She's a Mrs Parkhurst – says she knows you from when you were here sixteen years ago.

Flora Mrs Parkhurst? My old landlady in Heatherley!

Louie Heatherley?

Flora My name for Grayshott. How nice of her. And with her daughter, you say? How old would her daughter be?

Louie Bit younger than me, I'd say.

Flora Younger than you – then it must be Elsie, the one who was born just before I left. What a coincidence she should turn up with her late-comer

105

just now.

Louie Shall I ask then to come through?

Flora Please Louie.

But Mrs Parkhurst bursts in without ceremony, with Elsie in tow,
as Louie exits

Mrs Parkhurst Flora, here you are!

Flora *(Rising, a little awkwardly)* Mrs Parkhurst – how nice to see you.

Mrs Parkhurst Oh, none of that 'Mrs Parkhurst' – I'm not your landlady now – call me Florrie – we're both mothers with families – grandmother myself several times over. But what do you think of my little Lammas lamb? D'you see any change in her?

Flora If I'd not been told, I wouldn't have recognised her.

Mrs Parkhurst *(Laughing)* I don't suppose you would either.

Flora *(To Elsie)* You were pink and screaming in a nappy last time I saw you. I left your mother's house almost before you had your eyes open.

Elsie I know – mum's told me all about you.

Flora Oh dear – that sounds ominous.

Elsie What a one you were for books, and for bringing in great bunches of wild flowers …

Mrs Parkhurst And for running upstairs two at a time.

Flora I'm not sure I could do that now.

Mrs Parkhurst But you were always a great help to me – more help than all the male lodgers I'd had put together.

Flora And how is Mr Parkhurst?

Mrs Parkhurst Poor Mr Parkhurst, he passed away five years back, poor dear soul.

Flora Oh, I am sorry.

Mrs Parkhurst A truly Christian end, and so patient with it. But he loved Elsie – our daughter Elsie. The flower of the family, he called her. All the others have left home now, and I don't know what I'd do without her.

Flora I'm sure she's a great help.

Mrs Parkhurst She's the clever one of the family. She won a scholarship to secondary school. And tell Mrs Thompson what you're doing now Elsie.

Elsie I'm going to study book-keeping.

Mrs Parkhurst Book-keeping. She'll get good money in one of those hotels with that. She won't see her old mother want for anything, will you Elsie.

Flora You're looking very well, Mrs Parkhurst.

Mrs Parkhurst There you go, 'Mrs Parkhurst' again. D'you know, I feel younger now than I did when I had Elsie. Odd isn't it. Ever since the rest of the children left and gave me some time to myself. God has been kind to me though, Flora. Mr Parkhurst left me a small pension, and I've been able to move into a better house – with two front rooms to let to summer visitors.

Flora That sounds nice.

Mrs Parkhurst But Elsie, bless her heart, she'll see that we don't have to let rooms for ever, won't you dear. She'll see her old mum into a comfortable retirement. You've two children, your husband was saying.

Flora Yes, fourteen and eight now.

Mrs Parkhurst There, just the two. You young people don't have the large families we did. There's sense in that I suppose – not so many mouths to feed. But, you know, I'd do it all again if I had my time over. And you never really know when you've had the last – you might have a little surprise bundle arrive yet, like I did!

Flora *(Hesitant)* Yes.

Mrs Parkhurst Don't tell me ...! Not you too?

Flora *(Nodding)* A little surprise bundle. We heard yesterday.

Mrs Parkhurst Well, this is a day, to be sure. D'you hear that, Elsie? She'll be the pride of the family. Or he, of course. They say the un-expected ones are always the best.

Flora I hope so. With the war still on ...

Mrs Parkhurst Oh there'll be an end to this war before long – our children will see better times than we've had. This is the war to end all wars.

Flora I wish I could believe that.

Mrs Parkhurst Needed one like this to knock some sense into their heads.

Flora It cost my brother his life.

Mrs Parkhurst No! The one you were so glad to see come back from the other war? There's no justice in the world – I sometimes really do believe that. When's the little one due?

Flora In October, the same as Diana and Basil were.

Mrs Parkhurst Be all over bar the shouting by then. This 'tin town' or 'mudsplosh camp' or whatever it's called – here where all the Canadian troops are – that'll be cleared away and within a few years we'll have forgotten anything was ever there.

Elsie What will you call your baby, Mrs Thompson?

107

Mrs Parkhurst Good heavens Elsie, she's only just found out she's having it! You don't just come up with a name like that out of the blue.

Flora My husband will probably want to choose something with a political significance.

Mrs Parkhurst Whose side is he on?

Flora Oh the Liberals – that's one thing we have in common at least.

Mrs Parkhurst Well, it takes all sorts I suppose. Never talk politics or religion in polite company, they say.

Flora No. Will you stay for tea?

Mrs Parkhurst I wouldn't say no, would you, Elsie? She's so much to tell you about how she's getting on, our daughter Elsie, *(to Elsie)* haven't you dear. You just can't stop her. Yes, a cup of tea would be very nice … .

Scene 14

A street in Liphook, at the same time

Sgt Mumford and Louie enter from opposite directions – she with her bicycle

Sgt Mumford Hi, Postie.

Louie I didn't expect to see you here, not this time of day.

Sgt Mumford I was waiting for you – thought you'd be passing by about now.

Louie What's this then – hoping to mend my puncture again?

Sgt Mumford Something like that.

Louie All right today though – my tyres.

Sgt Mumford You won't get into trouble then – being late back to the office, I mean.

Louie I know what you mean.

Sgt Mumford I guess you do.

Louie Did you let them down on purpose that first time?

Sgt Mumford I did not.

Louie Your first day in the country.

Sgt Mumford And today's my last.

Louie Your last?

Sgt Mumford Our orders have come through. We're moving out tomorrow.

Louie Oh.

Sgt Mumford So it'll be goodbye Merrie England for a while, and goodbye

Postie Woods.

Louie Where are you …

Sgt Mumford No idea where – but they won't be sending us out there to play baseball.

Louie You'll write, won't you.

Sgt Mumford I'll write it – you deliver it.

Scene 15

Flora's room, Liphook Post Office, at the same time

Flora is still with Mrs Parkhurst and Elsie

Flora It's been lovely seeing you again Mrs Parkhurst …

Mrs Parkhurst Florrie.

Flora Florrie – and you too Elsie.

Mrs Parkhurst She's a proper chatterbox this one. You've heard all about us and we've hardly had a word about you.

Flora There's nothing much to tell really. Got married, two children, a third on the way …

Mrs Parkhurst *(Rising)* Well it's nice to know you're happy dear, after all this time. You must come over and see us.

Flora Yes – I probably will – when the war's over, and after I've stopped changing nappies again …

Mrs Parkhurst They're worth it though – just look at Elsie – our daughter Elsie. I'll admit I was taken aback at the time, you remember don't you, but now I can truly say she was worth every minute of time and trouble I spent on her. *(To Elsie)* Every minute, weren't you dear.

Flora I'm glad. Well, goodbye then – and goodbye Elsie.

Elsie Goodbye Mrs Thompson. Glad to have met you.

Mrs Parkhurst She is too – been talking about you ever since I found out you were living here. No need to see us out, dear – we can go back though the shop. See you before long I hope.

Mrs Parkhurst and Elsie exit

Scene 16

Split scene: Flora and Louie

Flora watches Mrs Parkhurst and Elsie go as Louie watches Sgt Mumford go

Flora Before long. I thought I'd have some time to myself before long.

Louie Take care of yourself.

Flora Sorting, queuing, shopping, cooking, with a little sleeping and writing squeezed in between – and now come the autumn …

Louie Write to me.

Flora Come the autumn, back to nappies and night feeds.

Louie Goodbye and good luck. Don't forget. See you in a few weeks when you come back.

Flora Goodbye famous village author – don't flinch – you'll have to wait a few more years yet.

Music: 'Goodbye-ee'

– INTERVAL –

An Advertisement for Correspondence Courses, 1925

Can You Write?

IF SO, DO NOT BURY YOUR TALENT, but have it trained by means of one of our Courses.

SHORT STORY WRITING.

Complete Course of Six Lessons, with revision of Pupil's own efforts and advice as to placing with Editors.

CONDUCTED BY

FLORA THOMPSON, Author of 'Bog-Myrtle and Peat,' 'The Peverel Papers,' &c, AND

MYLDREDE HUMBLE-SMITH, Honours English Language and Literature, Oxon., B.Litt., Durham.

Terms for the Full Course £1 10 6 (Instalments arranged if desired).

THOSE WHO DO NOT ASPIRE TO WRITE FOR THE PRESS SHOULD OBTAIN PARTICULARS OF OUR GENERAL CULTURE COURSE

POETS ARE INVITED TO JOIN THE PEVEREL SOCIETY.

All Particulars may be obtained from: MISS FLORA THOMPSON Ruskin House, Liphook, Hants.*

This scene could be achieved by reading out or displaying or handing out a copy of Flora's actual advertisement to the audience during the interval.

Scene 17

An open space near Liphook, summer 1926

Bill & Maggie Tidy enter

Maggie You can't stop 'ere, Bill Tidy. They'll move us on if we stops 'ere, you knows that.

Bill Let 'em. Here I stops and here I has me pipe and me dinner. Where's me 'baccy gone?

Maggie You stay then. I'm not waiting. We've had trouble enough with the author'ties, you knows that.

Bill What author'ties? We got rights – this 'ere's a public way. You can stay for two nights and a day without interference on a public way.

Maggie They'll still move us on.

Bill They can't. It's a law immemorial.

Maggie You using language again?

Bill Immemorial. That means carved out on stone, like in the Bible.

Maggie Where is it then, this stone?

Bill Oh I dunno. Up in Lunnun somewhere I shouldn't wonder. 'Swhere all them laws come from. Now are you gettin' me my dinner, Mrs Tidy, or ain't you?

Maggie Always fretful you are.

Flora enters at a distance

Bill Good cause to be. Oh lor, see who's spotted us now.

Maggie The police?

Bill Worse – the woman who asks all them questions. P'raps you're right about moving on.

Maggie She's all right, the postmistress.

Bill Dunno when she gets to do any postmistressing – spends all her time walking on the commons. *(To Flora)* Aft'noon ma'am.

Flora Good afternoon, Bill. I'm glad I found you.

Bill We was just on our way.

Flora I was hoping you could tell me what this plant is. It's new to me.

Bill Dinner time.

Maggie That's not the name of the plant – that's why we're on our way.

Bill No offence, ma'am. It be hawkweed, as you can see. But there be hundreds of hawkweeds. This 'yun – now he be a new one on me too.

Maggie Not often you hears Mr Tidy saying that – new one on him too.

Bill No, bain't neither. Where did yer find 'im then?

Flora On the down. Just behind that clump of …

Diana (22) enters in haste

Diana Mother! Mother, found you – look what's come!

Flora Di, whatever's the matter?

Diana Look. From Australia. He's written.

Flora Really? Which one?

Diana Cecil! – but Basil sends his love too.

Flora Oh, good.

Bill Well, since you'se got company now, we'll be moving along. Good day to you ma'am. And to you miss.

Maggie Fancy that – a new one on Mr Tidy! *(They exit)*

Diana I thought he'd forgotten about me.

Flora Well, he's remembered enough to send a letter at least. How is he?

Diana Having a wonderful time, by the sound of it. *(Shows it to her)*

Flora Orange and lemon groves around the bungalow, pineapples and peaches as common as potatoes, banana plantations, hibiscus hedges … Well don't look so glum then – you want him to be happy, don't you?

Diana I want him to be here.

Flora Well, dear, we can't always have what we want when we want it – you know that.

Diana Mother, Cecil and I are engaged!

Flora I know, I know …

Diana And he's on the other side of the world. How would you like to be that far away from father and never see him for months – years perhaps?

Flora Oh, Di – what a question to ask!

Offstage, a gramophone starts to play 'I'm Forever Blowing Bubbles'

What on earth's that? Fancy bringing a gramophone out into the country!

Diana It's these Londoners – they come here for fresh air, and they can't stand the peace and quiet.

Flora What a din. Well each to his own, I suppose. What amuses me is watching them pick their way through all the brambles in their silk stockings and patent-leather shoes.

Diana Jealousy, mother!

Flora No such thing, Di. Can you imagine me wearing anything like that?

Or you for that matter.

Diana *(Teasing)* Speak for yourself! I'm past the age of consent now – I might surprise you by wearing a pair of silk stockings yet.

Flora On your wages as a telephone operator?

Diana They're not so bad. Any news of that night-operator being appointed yet?

Flora Your father thinks the Post Office will agree to it soon.

Diana Not before time. Then we can start looking for that little cottage you've always wanted to buy.

Flora Once he stops having to cover for the night shift, yes.

Diana Poor mother – you're a proper 'postmaster's widow' …

Flora Come on, Di – you know I don't mind it that much. It gives me time to write.

Diana The last thing you wrote was that new Guide Book for the village – you made such a good job of it, it's probably why we've got all these day-trippers here now.

Flora It's more likely due to the professors and politicians who used to live along the road. They made a far better job of advertising the countryside round here than I ever could.

Diana Including your friend, Sir Arthur Conan Doyle.

Flora Stop teasing me. He used to come and send telegrams from my post office, he and George Bernard Shaw, but I hardly spoke more than a dozen words to either of them.

Diana I can't believe it.

Flora Post office regulations, my girl – no fraternising with the customers. Anyway, I was too shy in those days. Not like you and your elder brother.

Diana Basil? He'd probably have asked for their autograph if he'd been around.

Flora Quite likely. *(A pause)* It's over four months now since they left.

Diana *(Fingering her engagement ring)* You don't need to remind me.

Flora And Basil not even sixteen yet. I just hope your Uncle Frank's keeping an eye on them. He was twenty-one when <u>he</u> emigrated there.

Diana Same age as Cecil. Do you think they'll ever come back?

Flora Have you ever known Basil stick at anything for longer than a year?

Diana I wasn't thinking of Basil so much. I was thinking of my fiancé.

Flora *(Non-committal)* Yes.

Diana I sometimes don't think you and father approve of him.

Flora Oh, Di. If only life were so straight forward.

Diana *(Determined to change the subject)* Let's hope the night-operator job gets approved – then you can concentrate your mind on moving. It'll be nice not having to live next to the job any more.

Flora I've heard there's a new house being built at Griggs Green.

Diana Right by your Peverel Down. Sounds ideal – how much is it?

Flora I've no idea. But I've asked your father to find out.

Diana Shall we walk over there now, and see what it looks like?

Flora Have you got time before your afternoon shift?

Diana I start again at four-thirty, so we should just about manage it – if we don't dawdle.

Flora You mean, if I don't stop to look at too many things on the way.

Diana Something like that.

Scene 18

In Liphook Post Office, a few days later

John Thompson is talking to Joe Leggett, now eighteen

John A penny'th of gob-stoppers is it, Joe Leggett?

Joe Beg pardon, Mr Thompson?

John I was just remembering back about ten years or so when I first met you.

Joe Oh, the gob-stoppers – yes.

John What can I do for you today?

Joe I'd like some money out of my savings, please.

John Withdrawal from Savings Account, eh? Right. Have you got your book?

Joe Yes – it's here. *(Hands it over)*

John I see – and this is your first withdrawal. How much would you like to take out?

Joe Two shillings.

John Two shillings. Thinking of buying the Crown Jewels?

Joe No, not quite.

John Well now, for withdrawals you have to fill in this form. *(Hands form to him)* There's a pen over there.

Joe nods and takes the form to one side

And remember to sign it at the bottom.

Harry Envis enters behind the counter

Harry Fishing tomorrow, Mr Thompson?

John I think so, Harry, yes.

Harry Should be a good day for tench if this weather holds. Nice warm, still weather – just what they like.

John Have to be an early start then.

Harry Want to be there at daybreak for the best chance.

John I'll have Flora pack me a lunch tonight.

Harry Bread paste on a No. 6 hook.

John Pardon? Oh, what you're using for bait. You think so?

Harry Aye – but I'll take my worms as well, just in case. See you down at the Mere then. *(Exits)*

Joe approaches with his completed form

Joe I've signed it.

John *(Takes the form)* Let me have a look. *(Sucks his teeth)* I'm sorry, Mr Leggett – you've filled in two shillings in words, but two pounds in figures. Look – d'you see? *(He shows him)* I'm afraid I'll have to get you to do another.

Joe Can't I just change it?

John Best do it properly *(Getting him a fresh form)* Oh, and just a minute – you've signed in the wrong place too – that's where I'm supposed to countersign it. Lucky I noticed, or you'd have had to fill in a third one.

Joe I see.

John Here, let me watch you.

Joe *(Filling it in)* So the two goes in that column.

John That's right. And your signature goes there.

Joe *(Handing it to him)* Is that all right?

John That's correct. And now I countersign it – and hand you back your book with your withdrawal marked on it – and finally, give you your two shillings.

Joe Thank you.

John So now you'll know how to do it next time. There's nothing to these things if you just take the time to read the forms.

Joe Yes I'm sure. Well, goodbye.

John Goodbye Mr Leggett.

Joe exits

Ten years ago it was gob-stoppers, now I'm spending my time issuing two-shilling savings withdrawals. Where have you gone wrong, John Thompson?

Scene 19

The garden of the Postmaster's House, a few weeks later

Flora is trying her hand at water divining – Peter, age 8, enters

Peter Mother! What are you doing?

Flora I'm trying my hand at water divining.

Peter What's that?

Flora An old way of finding water underground.

Peter I thought it came from a tap.

Flora When I was your age, Peter, there was none of this turning a tap indoors to get water – we had to go outside and get it from a well or a pump.

Peter How far away was that?

Flora It depended. Some lucky folk had one in their garden – others had to walk to the middle of the village. A water diviner could tell you where to dig your well.

Peter Sounds like magic. Can I try?

Flora *(Hands him the forked hazel rod)* Have a go – this is where the old well for the house used to be, so I thought I might find something here.

Peter tries it for a while

Peter What's it supposed to do?

Flora I'm told it should quiver if you walk over water.

Peter I can't feel anything.

Flora Nor could I – but I saw a man using one yesterday. He walked around for nearly an hour, then suddenly stopped and said, 'Just there, at the depth of seven feet, you will find!' – and I'm told when they dug, they hit a spring exactly where he'd said.

Peter Do they still dig wells then?

Flora Yes, where there's no mains water. We had no electricity or gas either when I was a girl.

Peter How did you see at night?

Flora Candles if you could afford them – most folk in the village used rush lights – I must have made thousands of them in my time. Rushes peeled and dipped in fat.

Peter Peeled?

Flora You had to leave a strip unpeeled to support the pith. Burned for about an hour if you made a good one.

Peter I bet they were smelly.

Flora We didn't really notice. Most people went to bed soon after nightfall and got up with the sun – that way we didn't have to worry so much about lighting.

Peter Would you like to live that way again?

Flora I really don't know. It seems long ago to me now, but there are plenty of people living around this village today who still have no gas, water or electricity. Haven't you heard them say so at school?

Peter We don't talk about that sort of thing.

Flora Oh? What sort of thing do you talk about then?

Peter Cars and aeroplanes.

Flora You've never seen an aeroplane.

Peter There's pictures in magazines. And my friend Charles knows somebody whose uncle owns a car.

Flora Does he now. He must have a lot of money.

Peter His uncle must.

Flora Personally, I enjoy going out on bus rides. It's cheaper and you don't have to learn how to drive.

Peter Be easy to drive a car.

Flora Well perhaps you're more mechanically minded than I am. I just like looking at the names on the front of the buses and imagining – Haslemere and Fernhurst; Milland and Forest Mere – good mouth-filling ready-made poetry, those names.

Peter Dad fishes at Forest Mere. D'you think he'll take me one day?

Flora You'd have to be up at crack of dawn, my lad, and keep quiet all day. I expect you'd be too much of a fidget for him.

Peter Not fair. How did he learn?

Flora Sea fishing off the Isle of Wight, I should think. It's a bit different.

Diana bursts in

Diana Has he agreed?

Flora I think so.

Diana You *think* so?

Flora Well, almost certainly. There are still a few I's to be dotted and T's to be crossed, but …

Diana So we'll be moving!

Flora If it all goes through, yes.

Peter Moving where?

Diana Down to a cottage.

Peter Nobody told me.

Flora We didn't want you to be disappointed if it all fell through.

Peter What sort of cottage? How big is it?

Flora Three bedrooms, two downstairs living rooms, a bathroom, kitchen, scullery and pantry.

Peter Is it old?

Diana No – it's only just been built.

Peter We won't have to go and get water from a well then.

Flora Not from a well – we have to get it from a pump.

Peter Outside?

Flora Yes. Quite like old times.

Peter *(Disappointed)* Oh, mother!

Diana But it's right by a farm, Peter – you can look at the animals next door. And outside the back gate there's the whole of Peverel Down to wander over.

Peter Silly! It's Weavers Down – even I know that.

Diana Mother calls it Peverel.

Peter I've heard her. *(To Flora)* Why don't you call things by their proper names?

Flora There's no easy answer to that. Sometimes another name just feels right.

Diana Anyhow, the house is called Woolmer Gate – *(to Peter)* is that good enough for you?

Flora Right on the edge of an old royal hunting forest – where kings and queens have come for thousands of years to enjoy the open air.

Diana I've a feeling we'll hardly see mother at home once we move there – she'll be out walking every moment of the day.

Flora I think there'll be a few other things to occupy my time. The garden for instance. A garden is one person's full-time job, or should be.

Peter Are there trees to climb?

Flora And looking after a mischievous son will take time too.

Diana It'll be far more relaxing than being in the middle of the village though.

Flora I think so. I'm looking forward to it very much. I only hope your father is too!

Scene 20

Liphook Post Office, at the same time

John Thompson serves Capt. Byfield

Capt. Byfield Bit quieter for you now, eh Thompson? Remember tales of when you had the Canadian and British camps here during the war.

John That was a busy time and no mistake.

Capt. Byfield Short staffed and under pressure, I'll be bound. Wasn't around here at the time myself, of course.

John I'm sure it was the same everywhere. But we hardly knew whether to laugh or cry when the war stopped. The 'flu epidemic took up to ten lives a day here.

Capt. Byfield Worrying time.

John Worst of it was, my wife had just had a baby.

Capt. Byfield Young Peter – he seems to have come through well enough.

John Gave us some worrying nights though, I can tell you.

Capt. Byfield Now we just have to worry about General Strikes and the like.

John Well, hopefully that's over and done with now.

Capt. Byfield Will those letters get to London first thing tomorrow?

John They'll catch the last collection tonight, yes. That's fourpence ha'penny for the three please, Capt Byfield.

Capt. Byfield *(Handing over money)* Do you never feel yourself wanting to move on, Thompson, to something bigger and better than a sleepy Hampshire village?

John It's a pleasant part of the world. I confess I miss being near to the sea – I grew up by the coast, and we were at Bournemouth before, you know – but my wife seems to like it here.

Capt. Byfield And the rest of the family?

John My daughter's got herself engaged to a local boy.

Capt. Byfield You sound slightly disapproving.

John Do I? Girls these days will do much as they please, it seems.

Capt. Byfield So she's unlikely to want to move.

John We'll see. The boy in question's gone to Australia, with my elder son.

Capt. Byfield The land of opportunity.

John So they think.

Capt. Byfield Well, it's our gain if you stay on here. Don't know a better-run post office around these parts.

John Thank you. But we'll be here a while longer I imagine – I've just been persuaded to buy a new house at Griggs Green.

Scene 21

On Weavers Down soon after

Flora is out walking. Suddenly Sam the shepherd appears.

Sam Lost, are you?

Flora I beg your pardon?

Sam No, just lost in your thoughts by the looks o' it.

Flora I'm sorry.

Sam No need – there's no crime in thinking. 'Bout the only thing they can't stop us doin' these days. Goin' far?

Flora Just over Peverel.

Sam I see. Now I've only lived here all me life, but I've never heard of a place by that name.

Flora No, it's an expression we use in the family.

Sam Ah, family too. Look too young to have a family.

Flora Your eyes deceive you, I'm afraid.

Sam Nothing wrong with my eyes, young lady. Can't be a shepherd 'less you can spot yer critters when they're well away.

Flora Are there sheep here?

Sam What would a shepherd be a'doin' of with no sheep?

Flora I've no idea.

Sam The flock's all around you, look. Southdowns.

Flora I see.

Sam Best make the most of today though. Weather's on the turn.

Flora The forecast was good.

Sam I carries me weather glass about me. It's just here in my right shoulder blade. Let's you know when rain's around twenty-four hours beforehand.

Flora Then I must remember to put on something waterproof tomorrow.

Sam Aye, that's about the only good thing that be said of Rheumatics – you knows when to leave your topcoat at home and when to bring it along.

Flora I must get on. I'm keeping you from your flock.

Sam So you are – and I'm keeping you from your Peverel, wherever that may be. *(As she exits)* Remember your coat the 'morrow. *(To himself)* What's a young female critter with a family doing, walking out in all weathers? Don't seem natural somehow. Don't even let my sheep do that.

Scene 22

The Leggett's farm, Griggs Green, a few weeks later

Joe Leggett is talking to his mother

Joe They seem to have settled in all right next door.

Mrs Leggett The postmaster and his family? I hope you've not been going poking your nose in there, Joe Leggett.

Joe No – just looking as I go past.

Mrs Leggett She seems to be a 'lady', but her husband's no 'gentleman'.

Joe What do you mean?

Mrs Leggett Just my judgement.

Joe He's a bit of a stickler for the rules they say, but he's very fair.

Mrs Leggett That may well be.

Joe Have you spoken to them?

Mrs Leggett She came round to buy some milk and eggs from us yesterday. Just the usual talk about the weather from her. I've not spoken to him – not socially that is.

Joe Only in the post office.

Mrs Leggett And not too impressed with him there.

Joe I know how to fill the forms in now.

Mrs Leggett Yes, I'll wager you do, but what good's that to man or beast?

Joe Talking of beasts, I'd better be getting the herd down for milking.

Mrs Leggett I wonder what they think, with all the farm noise here in the early hours? I expect they thought it would be all peace and quiet.

Joe I reckon Mrs Thompson knows a bit about the countryside – I've seen her talking to old Sam the shepherd often enough.

Mrs Leggett Him and his imaginary flock of sheep. I wonder what stories he tells her.

Joe And the number of times she's caught me bird-nesting on her walks in the past.

Mrs Leggett Has she indeed? She won't have a very good opinion of you then.

Joe I don't think she recognises me from that long ago. Anyhow I was only looking – I didn't touch the eggs. *(He exits)*

Mrs Leggett *(After him)* Just as well. That reminds me. *(Calls)* Eileen, are you there? Fetch the eggs in from the hens would you please.

Eileen enters – she is about 16 years old

And when you've collected them, take half a dozen round next door – I promised Mrs Thompson she could have some more.

Scene 23

In 'Woolmer Gate', Griggs Green, soon after

Diana returns from her shift at the post office telephone exchange

Flora How was the post office today?

Diana It seems strange having to ask, after all that time living next door.

Flora Yes.

Diana You'll be glad to know the post office is fine, and I've handed the switchboard over to father for the night. It's a pity the new appointment still hasn't come through.

Flora He didn't know that when we agreed to buy the house.

Diana Just as well perhaps, or we might never have moved. I see you've made a start in the garden.

Flora Yes. I should have been organising my study, but it was too nice to stay indoors.

Diana Where's Peter?

Flora Out exploring. Watching the work next door on the farm I should think.

Diana Not disturbing them I hope.

Flora I told him to stay our side of the fence. Pop your head out would you Di, and tell him it's time to come in now.

Diana *(Looking off-stage)* No need – he's coming now, with the egg-girl.

Flora He's bound to have forgotten that he's got a lot of homework to do.

Diana I'm glad I'm past that stage now.

> *Peter and Eileen enter – she is carrying eggs*

(To Peter) I was just about to call you in.

Peter This is Eileen from next door.

Flora Oh that is kind of you to bring them round – I could easily have collected them.

Eileen It's really no trouble. They're fresh laid. Still warm.

Peter I met her coming over.

Diana Yes, Peter, so we saw.

Flora *(To Eileen)* How much do I owe you?

Eileen That's ninepence, please.

Flora I'll put these in the kitchen and get you some money. *(She exits)*

Eileen Settled in now, have you?

Diana It'll take a while longer before we feel we're really here.

Eileen You've not moved too far though.

Diana That's true. It's a short bike ride to work now instead of just walking through a connecting door.

Peter Where do your cows come from?

Eileen They graze up at the big farm on Weavers Down – we bring them down twice a day.

Peter Oh, up on Peverel.

Eileen Pardon?

Diana Just a family name. I'm afraid he'll be over and pestering you if you let him – he's fascinated by farms.

Eileen I'm sure mum and dad won't mind that.

Diana Don't let him get in your way though.

> *Flora re-enters with money*

Flora Ninepence – thank you very much.

Eileen There'll be more tomorrow if you'd like to come to the door. We do butter too.

Flora Thank you – I shall.

Peter Can I have a ride up the hill on your mule and cart?

Flora Peter!

Eileen *(Laughing)* That's my brother Joe's department. You'd best ask him.

Diana I'm sure he will.

Eileen Well, I must be getting back. I've still got work to do in the dairy.

Diana It must be a long day, working on the farm.

Eileen It is. Still, mustn't grumble. It's a job, and they're hard enough to come by these days. Good night, Mrs Thompson.

Flora Good night, Eileen.

Eileen Good night, young Peter. See you again, I've no doubt.

Eileen exits

Diana Who'd have a younger brother!

Flora I think you've some homework to do, haven't you Peter?

Peter I've done most of it.

Flora Well I'll be along to check shortly. Off you go.

Peter goes

Now, Di, you and I can relax for a while and listen to the new wireless set.

Diana If we can tune it in properly this time.

Flora I'll go and make some coffee and leave that to you.

Diana It's not time for your Choral Evensong, is it?

Flora No, that's at four o'clock on Thursday afternoons. I'm hoping there's a play on, and we might get the weather forecast.

Diana Hasn't old Sam the shepherd told you that already?

Flora Yes, but it will be interesting to see if the wireless gets it right! *(Exits)*

Scene 24

In Liphook Post Office, early morning a few weeks later

John Thompson has acted as night switchboard operator.
Harry Envis enters

John Good morning Harry.

Harry Morning, Mr Thompson. Had a good night on the switchboard?

John No calls at all. I suppose that's a good night.

Harry Been reading the *Post Office Circular* I see, to keep you awake.

John Not the most riveting of magazines, but better than nothing.

Harry Well, we can take over now if you want to get home.

John Is the sorting office fully manned?

Harry Aye, everybody present and correct and at their posts.

John Right – I'll just have a quick check in there myself, then I'll be off.

Harry Fishing on Sunday? Thought we'd try Waggoners Wells.

John Yes, for a change – that should be very pleasant.

Harry Got the choice of ponds there.

John *(About to exit)* Will you be bringing your festering rabbit on a stick?

Harry No. I'll leave him dropping maggots into Forest Mere for next time.

John One of these days, Harry, I'll get back to doing some proper fishing – in the sea! *(He exits)*

Harry *(To himself)* Proper fishing! I don't know! (*Picks up the Post Office Circular*) Not my taste in reading either. Hallo, what's this he's marked here? 'Applications sought for position of Postmaster in Dartmouth.' Well that's certainly near the sea. Ha – I wonder, could we be losing our Mr Thompson soon?

Scene 25

On Weavers Down, early spring 1927

Flora out walking carrying her camera, and observing nature as she goes.
She walks by old Sam the shepherd without noticing him.

Sam There you are, scurrying by again.

Flora *(Startled)* Oh, Sam – I didn't see you.

Sam Never do. Nor anything else, I'll be bound. On one o' your Peverel walks again, are you?

Flora I was just admiring the view and trying to take some photographs. The South Downs are so clear today.

Sam Be a wet 'un afore long though.

Flora Surely not.

Sam When you can hear the trains rush out o' Buriton tunnel, you know it means a wet 'un's on the way.

Flora How did we manage before there were railways?

Sam You can smell rain and taste rain for hours before it begins. And that 'oss's tail over the trees – that means 'weather' too.

Flora Never mind – I like to be out in anything.

Sam Then you'se obviously not a shepherd. Wind and cold you can fight – 'tis rain and fog be the enemies. Damp, muggy weather's the death o' ewes and lambs.

Flora Well, I'm dressed warmly enough for all weathers.

125

Sam Make sure you keeps your feet dry though – that's the danger – wet feet.

Flora I'll remember it. You're still carrying on, then?

Sam I've been 'carrying on' ever since my old father died forty years since. The farmer were always going to hire a new shepherd at the Heath Fair each year, but he never did. S'pose I must be doin' the job all right by now.

Flora I'm sure you are.

Sam Each year writes one more wrinkle on the shepherd's brow. *(Pause – Flora turns to go)* Now don't you rush away again 'afore I show you this.

Flora What is it?

Sam Over here, under the hedge – look.

Flora A primrose.

Sam Aye, a primrose.

Flora It's a bit thin and straggly though – too early really, I suppose.

Sam *(Disappointed)* Too early?

Flora *(Quickly)* But wonderful for the time of year.

Sam 'Tis but a primrose to you, a sight you'll see a many more times if you're spared as long as is natural. But when you're gettin' on in years like me, each time you see the like you know it might be your last, and you seems to set a value on it somehow.

Flora I think it's beautiful, Sam. Truly.

Sam Something more than a common flower – but there, I can't really explain it.

Flora You've explained it to me.

Sam 'Tis like, during the war when they ordered all them black-outs at night. I remember looking up at the full moon and the stars then and saying to myself: 'They can't put that out, nor the sun, nor the stars, for all their mightiness.' At bottom, it's the way the Lord intended.

Flora I'm sure that's right.

Sam Now, I must get back to my flock, and you must hurry on wherever you're a'going.

Flora Before I get my feet wet.

Sam Aye – 'tis no good female critters getting their feet wet, believe me.

Flora Thank you, Sam – I'll remember that. *(Exits)*

Sam Just a primrose. A poor, leggy primrose.

Scene 26

The Telephone Exchange, Liphook Post Office

Diana is showing Eileen how to be an operator

Eileen I'm so grateful to you and your mother, Di, for getting me this job.

Diana You can thank father for appointing you.

Eileen I don't think I'd have been his first choice! I imagine your mother pulled a few strings.

Diana I think she usually gets her way with father – even if he doesn't like to admit it.

Eileen It's a better future for me, being a telephone operator rather than a dairymaid.

Diana I think so. Look – there's a call coming in now – will you take it?

Eileen Right. *(Plugging in)* Number please. *(Pause)* Yes I *am* new here – oh, hello Mrs Moss, it's Eileen Leggett – thank you, yes very much – the Green Dragon? I'll try to connect you. *(To Diana)* It's Mrs Moss.

Diana The Green Dragon's engaged at the moment.

Eileen Is it? *(Checks her board)* Oh yes. I'm sorry Mrs Moss, they're engaged at the moment. Shall I ring you back when they're free? Right-o – goodbye. *(Unplugs)*

Diana Well done – you'll make supervisor grade yet.

Eileen Do you often have chats like that with the subscribers?

Diana There are only about a hundred in the village – we get to know them quite well.

Eileen Yes, I should think so.

Diana Look – the Green Dragon's free now – you'd better ring Mrs Moss back.

Eileen Where? Oh yes, I see. *(Plugging in again)* Hello, Mrs Moss – the Dragon's free now – I'm ringing for you. That's all right, goodbye. *(Unplugs)*

Diana There, you're getting the hang of it.

Eileen What else do I need to know?

Diana You're helping me with the morning shift at first, working nine till twelve-thirty. Then if things go well you'll be given a full-time job later.

Eileen I think I'll enjoy it. *(Pause)* Have you heard from your brother in Australia lately?

Diana *(Off hand)* Not lately – nor from Cecil.

Eileen I'm sorry.

Diana *(Fingering her engagement ring)* I'm sure they'll write if there's anything worthwhile to say.

Eileen Yes.

Diana Meanwhile I keep myself busy and try not to think about it too much.

Scene 27

At 'Woolmer Gate', Griggs Green, soon after

John and Flora are gardening

Flora Those dahlias should be a mass of colour in the summer.

John Yes.

Flora And I thought we might try some delphiniums over there.

John Uh-huh.

Flora With the marigolds and nasturtiums – they'll make a splash of gold along the border.

John Yes, that'll be very nice.

Flora You don't sound very enthusiastic.

John Sorry. No, they'll be lovely.

Flora Your mind's not on gardening today is it, I can see that.

John I'm not sure we should overdo the planting this year.

Flora I want to get things sorted out. If we wait till next year we may never do it.

John No.

Flora So why don't we dig another bed along here. John, are you listening?

John You're right – my mind's not on gardening.

Flora What, then?

John I've – applied for another job.

Flora I beg your pardon?

John Applied for another job.

Flora You mean – away from Liphook?

John In Devon – Dartmouth.

Flora You let us move here, then applied for another job?

John I'd been thinking about it for some time. It means promotion.

Flora John, you're 53 years old – you've only seven more years to go before compulsory retirement.

John Postmaster of a sizeable town – it's always been my ambition.

Flora And it's by the sea. You say you've *applied* for the job.

John I applied a while back – today I heard I'd been accepted.

Flora Accepted. And as a dutiful wife, I am expected to follow you with the family.

John But you can write anywhere. And you do all your correspondence by post now anyway.

Flora And much of my correspondence is about the joys of living in Hampshire.

John Well, now it can be about the joys of living in Devon.

Flora And the children?

John The children? With this so-called fiancé of Diana's in Australia with Basil, and not likely to come back, I should think she'd be glad to get away from the place. And Peter's too young to worry.

Flora I see.

John Gives that Dr Macfie a longer journey if he still wants to find you, I'm afraid. Haven't seen him for a while anyway.

Flora Perhaps he wasn't sure of his welcome.

John Perhaps he wasn't. Anyway, I'm sorry about the house.

Flora Thank you.

John I wasn't sure about the promotion, not until after we'd moved.

Flora No need to explain. I think I'll go and make the tea.

John Shall I finish the border.

Flora *(Exiting alone)* There doesn't seem to be much point now, does there.

Scene 28

Lynchmere Common

Bill & Maggie Tidy enter arguing

Maggie That's it then – if I had anywhere to go now I'd leave yer.

Bill Leave me? Huh! I'd be so lucky.

Maggie I dunno who's the biggest fool, Bill Tidy – you or the donkey. Least the donkey was sober last night.

Bill You'd had a few glasses yerself as well.

Maggie But I didn't try to light me pipe then, did I? And I didn't flick me

129

match-head into the tinder and see the 'ole lot go up in flames.

Bill You were right next to it though – if you been in yer senses you'd have put it out.

Maggie That's right, blame me.

Bill Stands to reason. You were the nearest.

Maggie Nearly set me on fire, you did, never mind the tent and everything else. All gone.

Bill Still got the cart.

Maggie Only 'cause the wind wasn't blowing that way. Nearly 'ad the donkey too.

Bill Always complaining, you are.

Maggie Complaining?

Bill Yes you are.

Maggie There's you saying "the King of England hisself couldn't turn us out, 'cause we've been here forty years" – and what happens? You burn us out in a single night.

Bill We can set up again. Just across the road there's some big hollies we can use. Bit of canvas hung up there and we'll be good as we were before.

Maggie With our beds and blankets in a big black smouldering heap over there? You may be lying on bare earth tonight, Bill Tidy, but I'm not.

Bill Where you plannin' on goin' then?

Maggie I don't rightly know yet – but I'll find somewhere, you see if I don't.

Bill Who's goin' to take a tinker's wife in?

Maggie I got friends – don't you go thinking I haven't.

Bill I can't think of any.

Maggie While you're sitting on your cart grinding away, I has a good old chat with all sorts. They all knows me.

Bill They wouldn't give you the time of day.

Maggie They all says, "Hallo Mrs Tidy, how are you today."

Bill If you was to ask them fer a bed fer the night, they'd run a mile.

Maggie There's my sister.

Bill Your sister's two days walk from here – thank God.

Maggie I'm not asking you to come.

Bill Wild horses wouldn't drag me.

Maggie So what are you goin' ter do then?

Bill I said. Scrap of canvas, an' I'll be right as rain.

Maggie You'd not look after yerself proper.

Bill Who says?

Maggie I knows you. After forty years I ought ter.

Bill Never had a chance to try.

Maggie Just as well, if you ask me.

Bill I wasn't asking yer.

Maggie No, but I knows all the same. They'd pick you up dead of starvation 'fore a week was up.

Bill Folks can live on *nothing* for longer than that.

Maggie You'd live on beer and nothing else.

Bill That's living then, ain't it? Darned if I know what you'se werritin' about, woman. Same as usual.

Maggie No, you always was higorant. Ever since I known you you'se been higorant. Don't know what I ever saw in you.

Bill So you're off then.

Maggie I will be.

Bill Taking anything?

Maggie There's nothing to take, Bill Tidy!

Bill 'Cept the donkey and cart. And the grindstone.

Maggie What would I do with the grindstone?

(Pause) We'd better get that canvas up then – looks like rain.

Bill Aye.

Maggie And some of that bedding – it might still do if I give it a good shake.

Bill Reckon it might.

Maggie And I'll cut a bit of heather and bracken ter go under us for tonight.

Bill Nothing wrong with sleeping on heather – nature's own fragrant bed.

Maggie Well – so are you goin' ter help me or not?

Bill Decided to stay then, have yer?

Maggie I said, are you goin' ter help?

Bill Only – if you're staying, I wouldn't say 'no' to a nice mug of tea!

Scene 29

The Leggett's farm, Griggs Green, a few weeks later

Joe Leggett is being watched by Peter

Peter Are you off up to Peverel again, Mr Leggett?

Joe You and your Peverel! Just as far as the big farm, yes.

Peter Can I come with you?

Joe If your mother doesn't mind, you can.

Peter She won't mind. She says she can get on with her work better when I'm not around.

Joe I see. What work's that, then?

Peter Oh, in her study – she doesn't like being disturbed.

Joe Well you can help me hitch the mule to the cart in a minute, then we'll go and see if we can find anything interesting to look at up on the hill.

Peter Is he old, your mule?

Joe Older than you. He's a war veteran – saw action against the enemy, he did.

Peter Did he get a medal?

Joe No, I'm afraid not. I hear you might be moving home again.

Peter Father's got a new job in Devon – but mother's staying here until we sell this house.

Joe Could take some time to do that, these days.

Peter That's what she's hoping.

Joe Pardon?

Peter She doesn't want to leave – but don't tell anyone else – I'm not supposed to know.

Joe Oh, I won't tell a soul. You know who you remind me of?

Peter No – who?

Joe That 'Just William' – the one who's in the magazine now.

Peter He's scruffy!

Joe Well, your hair's not quite so untidy as his, it's true.

Peter And I don't get into trouble like he does – at least, not often.

Joe I'm sure you don't. Come on, let's be off up to your Peverel. We'll give your mother a few hours peace and quiet from you.

132

Scene 30

Hewshott House, Liphook, summer 1927

Capt. Byfield is making a presentation to John Thompson

Capt. Byfield Well, Thompson, we're all sorry to see you leave, of course, after – what – eleven years among us now.

John Very kind of you to say so, Capt. Byfield.

Capt. Byfield You came during difficult times. It couldn't have been easy, but we all of us appreciate the efficient way in which you've run the post office here. Always found you courteous, obliging and willing to help whenever possible.

John I've always tried to be so.

Capt. Byfield I hope you'll be happy in your new posting – I'm sure you will – and we wish you every success. But we could not let you go without giving you some memento of your time in Liphook. So it gives me great pleasure to present you with this cheque for £40 and also a list of those who subscribed to it. *(Applause)* I'm sure these names will – if you'll excuse the pun – ring a bell with you when you look at them in years to come. *(More applause)*

Scene 31

At 'Woolmer Gate', Griggs Green, some time later

Flora is talking to Diana

Diana It seems odd without father here. Don't you mind not having a man in the house?

Flora I don't really think we'll be attacked in our beds, do you?

Diana I suppose he was never at home much during the night anyway. On his camp bed at the telephone exchange mostly.

Flora Yes – well, he seems to be settling in at Dartmouth now, and looking forward to us joining him.

Diana No more news from Basil?

Flora I'd tell you if I had. It would be nice to have him home, and see this house before we have to leave it.

Diana Nothing from Cecil either.

Flora Try not to let it get you down.

Diana I do.

Flora I had the man from the estate agent round today. They've advertised the house at £750.

Diana Was he optimistic?

Flora Not very.

Diana You're glad to say!

Flora You can think that, Di, but you're not supposed to say it. I told him we'd accept no offers less than £725 rock bottom. I shall plant up the garden and it will be a blaze of colour next summer. If we have to go, we'll go in style.

Diana Never flinch!

Flora That's right. But I'm afraid it will mean no more 'Peverel Papers' when we move.

Diana You've written one a month for the last five years or more – I should think you'd have run out of things to say by now.

Flora Not while I live here – there's so much to see on my walks, and characters to talk to, and history to read about …

Diana There must be all those things in Dartmouth too.

Flora Perhaps, but I feel it will be the end of an era when I leave Griggs Green.

Diana There's your novel.

Flora 'Gates of Eden'? Yes, I know – I've started it. Several times!

Diana But you've given it very little time while you've been here, what with Peverel this and Peverel that – not to mention ghost-writing for that big-game hunter.

Flora He reminded me of the conversations I'd had with old Mr Foreshaw in Heatherley, when I was your age.

Diana And then there's running the postal writers circle with Myldrede Humble-Smith.

Flora I've always said I would settle down and write a long novel, one day. Perhaps when we've moved …

Diana And meanwhile …

Flora Meanwhile – I ought to be getting Peter's tea ready before he gets home from school. I've told you about the maternal instinct of the female ant, haven't I?

Diana She nips off her wings so she can't fly away from her motherly duties.

Flora Yes. I sometimes think it would make a good text for a modern novel. Possibly autobiographical.

Diana Did you have any boyfriends before father came along?

Flora Some playmates and companions. Nobody serious.

Diana Really?

Flora Well – there was Richard when I was in Heatherley. He once told me he could never marry me. I remember thinking: 'Good Heavens, surely you don't think I want you to!'

Diana Didn't you?

Flora I honestly don't know. I think it happened at the wrong time for both of us – the wrong time to make a decision like that. He was short of money and his sister was very ill. I was about to leave Heatherley and didn't know what I'd be doing in the future.

Diana What did you say to him?

Flora I told him he didn't want to marry anyone just yet, and that by the time he did he'd have probably made himself a fortune.

Diana Did he? Make a fortune.

Flora I've no idea – we lost touch. Richard Brownlow – I wonder what happened to him?

Diana I wonder if it's the right time for me?

Flora With Cecil?

Diana He thinks he needs to earn money too, before he's ready for me. But perhaps he doesn't really want to marry anybody.

Flora But you're engaged to him – it's different surely.

Diana Perhaps – but I think I know how you felt with Richard.

Scene 32

At 'Woolmer Gate', Griggs Green, autumn 1928

John Thompson has returned to supervise moving out.
Peter is helping him, carrying a small packing case clearly marked
PLEASE KEEP DRY.

John Peter, will you please be careful with that – it's breakable.

Peter It's very light.

John Well don't say I didn't warn you. Where are you taking it?

Peter Outside.

John Can't you read boy?

Peter Read what?

John *(Indicating the packing case)* On the side?

135

Peter reads the message

It's been bucketing with rain out there from first light – where were you thinking of putting it?

Peter Ready for the van men to pick it up.

John I'm paying the removal firm to move everything out of the house. I know you're trying to be helpful, but just leave it there for them will you? There's nowhere dry to put it outside at the moment. Lord, what a day to choose to move!

Flora enters

Flora When's the taxi due?

John Any time now. Are you all ready?

Flora As ready as we'll ever be.

John Peter, leave it I said! I'm beginning to wish we'd sent you on ahead with Basil.

Peter I'm only trying to …

John Leave it!

Flora Let's hope the weather's better when we get to Dartmouth.

John Couldn't be much worse. Where's Diana?

Flora Just finishing her packing.

John She's been like a bear with a sore head these last few days.

Flora I think that's understandable, don't you?

John Never thought much of the fellow myself – she ought to be glad she's rid of him.

Flora I had a soft spot for Cecil. We all make mistakes you know.

John Don't know what you mean by that. Ah, here's the taxi now. Peter, go and tell your sister it's time to leave. *(Peter exits)*

Flora What a shame we have to see it for the last time looking like this. The lawn's a swamp and the flower borders are all bedraggled in the rain.

John Can't be helped. Now have you got what you're going to carry with you?

Flora Yes, but I'd just like to have a last look at Prince's grave before we go.

John We haven't time for that, woman! Besides, you'll get soaked.

Flora A soaking's nothing – clothes soon dry, but memories last somewhat longer.

John Right, the children are out there. Just pick up your things, Flora, and let's get in the taxi.

Flora Yes John.

John The sooner we're sitting in a warm, dry train, the happier I shall be. Goodbye Griggs Green. *(He exits)*

Flora Goodbye Peverel. *(She follows him)*

Music, slide projection or newsreadings to point up elapsed time

Scene 33 – April 1937

Richard Brownlow's retirement presentation

Chairman Richard Brownlow, you have had a remarkable career of over 40 years with our company. Starting at the bottom rung, as a Probationer at Porthcurno, you quickly progressed in our Far East division serving in Madras, Singapore and Hong Kong among other places, before returning home to take up your senior post here at head office. And we must not forget your distinguished war record in the Royal Engineers, for which of course you gained your OBE.

Now, on the occasion of your retirement, it is my pleasant duty to present you with this gift from your colleagues. Not, I may add, the usual piece of domestic plateware or a timepiece, but knowing your love of old printed works they have chosen to add some of these to your collection.

Applause as he hands over a portfolio of prints to Richard.

We wish you a long and happy retirement in the peace and seclusion of the cottage which I understand you have bought for yourself overlooking a quiet valley near the coast.

Light switches to Peter reading a magazine at home.

Peter Here's what I was telling you about, mother. The picture of the new liner that's just been launched.

Flora enters

Flora You must get this love of boats from your father, not from me.

Peter I enjoy being an engineer – in Dartmouth that means working with boats. Are you going to have a look at this or not?

Flora Show me then. *(She looks, then stares)*

Peter No, not that page mother – this one.

Flora *(Reading)* 'Retirement from cable company of Richard Brownlow'!

Peter Who's he?

Flora 'Hopes to spend a well-earned retirement in his cottage on the coast.'

Peter An old flame of yours?

Flora And no mention of a Mrs Brownlow sharing it with him.

Peter One of your dark secrets, mother?

Flora No, Peter. No dark secret. One of the paths that might have been, I suppose. We all have those. *(Reflectively)* I had a brother who was heading for a new life in Canada, until fate cut him down in Belgium three years before you were born.

Peter Uncle Edwin.

Flora The uncle Edwin you never knew. The Mrs Brownlow I never was. I wonder if Richard would have been just another dodder person.

Peter Pardon?

Flora 'The dodder cannot help being dodder – it was made that way.'

Peter I think I'll stick to engineering – it seems more straightforward somehow.

Flora Perhaps. When I lived in Lark Rise, life seemed straightforward – or at least it had an established rhythm. But since the time I was your age …

Peter Old people always think things were better in the old days.

Flora Not so much of the old! I may be nearly sixty, but there's a few years left in me yet.

Peter Then why don't you write about your times in Lark Rise? You're a writer.

Flora I'm still not sure your father believes that.

Peter But you are.

Flora I'd be trying to remember things as they were fifty years ago – in a hamlet on a gentle rise in the flat, wheat-growing north-east corner of Oxfordshire …

Peter When times were so much better than today.

Flora Not always, and never for some. We've gained a lot since those days, but we've lost a great deal too. Were you reading that magazine for a reason?

Peter I'm revising for my apprenticeship exam.

Flora Then you'd better get back to it. I've got supper to make, and then perhaps I can get back to this writing which you say I'm always doing.

Peter turns to do this

But keep the article on Richard for me, will you?

Scene 34 – May 1947

John Thompson faces the audience

John Was I the dodder in her life? If so, she found success despite me. How many of us make the perfect match anyway? I'll admit I was mindful of my work as postmaster, and as breadwinner. There's no wrong in that. To do a job well takes your full attention – and I either do a job well or not at all. There's no satisfaction in it otherwise, and we all look for satisfaction in our lives.

So, yes, it surprised me when she suddenly became a household name at the age of nearly 65. I was glad for her – and, I'll own, a little bit proud too. Then just as she was tasting success, young Peter went down in that Atlantic convoy. It was devastating – to both of us of course – but she'd also lost her brother in the other war. It was very hard for her then, but she persisted with her writing to the end, even though her health was going downhill. She finished the *Lark Rise* trilogy and finally completed *Still Glides the Stream*.

That was her swan song. On the 21st of May I'd been away all day on business. I came back in the evening and saw there was no meal on the table – feared the worst and rushed upstairs, but she was awake in bed – said she'd had one of her attacks at midday, but now she felt better. She asked me for a cup of tea – really quite cheerful she was – felt much better – so after a while I went downstairs again. I was only away from her for about an hour – then when I came back … gone.

I was stunned – I still feel quite ill about it.

We had her cremated and her ashes laid to rest at a spot she loved well.

The gypsy was right. She'll be loved by people she's never seen and never will see.

And I shall miss her!

— THE END —

Appendix A – Edited Calendar of Events

1876   Dec 5: Flora Jane Timms born in Juniper Hill, Oxfordshire.

1884   Professor John Tyndall builds first house at Hindhead, encouraging other 'eminent men' to follow.

1892   Walter Chapman takes Grayshott post office.

1897   October: Arthur Conan Doyle moves into *Undershaw*.

1898   June: George Bernard Shaw (GBS) spends his honeymoon at *Pitfold House*, near Hindhead.
Sept: Flora arrives in Grayshott and lodges with the Chapmans.
Nov: GBS rents *Blen Cathra* (now St Edmund's School), Hindhead.

1899   Jan 28: GBS delivers 'vigorous oration' at a Peace Meeting in Hindhead Congregational Hall – Conan Doyle in the chair also spoke.
Mar: Flora moves lodgings to 'Mrs Parkhurst'.
Aug 23: *Fox & Pelican* opens in Grayshott – Flora orders her 'immense ninepenny dinners' from it.
Flora starts seeing 'Mr Foreshaw' about this time?
Oct 10: Second Boer War begins.
Flora's brother Edwin *[Edmund in her books]* enlists for Boer War – meets Flora on Aldershot Railway Stn.

1900   Jan 6: Boers attack Ladysmith.
May 17: Mafeking relieved.
Aug 10: John Volckman *[Mr Foreshaw?]* dies at Grayshott, aged 63 – buried in Headley churchyard.
Sep: Hindhead telegraph facility opens.
At some date between September 1900 and March 1901, Flora leaves Grayshott.

1901   Jan 22: Queen Victoria dies.
Mar 31: Census: Flora is at Yateley post office; John Thompson is at Aldershot.
Jul 29: Walter Chapman murders his wife Emily at Grayshott and is committed to Broadmoor.

1903   Jan 7: Flora marries John Thompson at St Mary's, Twickenham.
Thompsons make home in Winton, a suburb of Bournemouth.
Oct 24: Winifred Grace ('Diana') Thompson born in Winton.

1909   Oct 6: Henry Basil Thompson born in Winton.

1910   Jan 12: Annie Symonds marries Harold Oliver Chapman (nephew of Walter) at St Luke's, Grayshott.

1912   Flora wins prize for writing a crit. on Dr Ronald Macfie's ode on the sinking of the *Titanic*.
Macfie visits Flora, and starts a literary correspondence.

1916	Apr: Flora's brother Edwin killed in action in Belgium.
	Aug: Thompson family moves from Bournemouth to Liphook.
1918	Oct 19: Peter Redmond Thompson born in Liphook.
1921	Book of Flora's poems published: *Bog Myrtle & Peat*.
1922	Flora begins writing her 'Peverel Papers' nature notes.
	Sept: Basil Thompson starts at Churchers College, Petersfield.
1923	Peter Thompson starts school (age 5)
1925	Flora helps to write the *Guide to Liphook*.
1926	Feb: Basil Thompson and Cecil Cluer (engaged to Diana) go out to Flora's brother Frank's farm in Queensland
	Thompsons buy *Woolmer Gate* at Griggs Green.
1927	July 6: Vacancy for postmaster at Dartmouth advertised.
	Aug 3: Appointment of John Thompson to Dartmouth recorded.
	Sep 9: *Woolmer Gate* put on the market.
	Nov: John Thompson moves to Dartmouth – Flora, Diana & Peter stay behind in Griggs Green to sell the house.
	Dec: Last 'Peverel Paper' appears.
1928	Autumn: Thompsons move from Griggs Green.
1931	Ronald Macfie dies.
1935	John Thompson retires.
1937	April: William Elwes *[Richard Brownlow]* retires.
1938	'Lark Rise' accepted by the Oxford University Press (OUP).
1939	Mar: 'Lark Rise' published.
	Flora starts writing 'Over to Candleford'.
1940	Mar: The Thompsons move from Dartmouth to Brixham.
1941	Sept: Peter Thompson lost at sea, aged 22.
1942	Flora writes 'Candleford Green'.
1943	Jan: 'Candleford Green' published.
1944	Flora writes 'Heatherley' but doesn't send it to OUP.
1945	Apr: Trilogy of 'Lark Rise to Candleford' published.
	Flora starts writing 'Still Glides the Stream'.
1946	Aug: 'Still Glides the Stream' completed.
1947	May 21: Flora dies in bed in the evening, aged 70.
1948	Jul 13: John Thompson dies, aged 74.

Appendix B – Characters in the plays

Cast of Flora's Heatherley, Grayshott 1998

Flora – In *Heatherley*, a young, gauche, country girl passing, as she says, "from foolish youth to wicked adolescence". In *Peverel*, a married lady with a husband and children of her own, hoping, against the odds, to "win the fight to write."

Walter Chapman – Born in Hertfordshire (hence Flora's pseudonym of 'Mr Hertford' for him?). In Grayshott he traded as Joiner and Cabinet Maker, running the village post office as 'a sideline to supplement his main income.' Flora says he was 'a dark, slightly-built man of forty-five who might have been thought handsome but for the peculiar tint of his complexion, which was a deep, dull mauvish-leaden shade, and the strange wild light in his eyes.' He had a 'disquieting habit of quoting texts of scripture or lines from the poets in a hissing whisper.' The Chapman family today cannot verify Flora's story of Walter's unrequited love for 'Letty', but they can confirm that he visited Australia on several occasions. They are not sure about 'heat-stroke' being the cause of his unstable mental condition in later life—another family legend blames a glass lemonade bottle which exploded in his face sending a sliver into his brain.

Emily Chapman – Married Walter on 13th November 1892 in All Saints' Church, Headley, which was the parish church of Grayshott at the time. He was 36 years old, she was 28. He murdered her on the morning of Monday 29th July 1901.

Ernest Chapman – Brother of Walter; he had come to the district before Walter, in about 1885, and started a building firm. He was a staunch Congregationalist.

Annie Symonds – Arrived in the village in November 1892 from her native Cheshire at the age of fourteen, when her father came down with Mr Marshall Bulley, related to the founder of Bees Seeds, to be his gardener at Hindhead. Later married Walter Chapman's nephew and ran the post office in the neighbouring village of Beacon Hill.

Charles Foreshaw – We are not sure who Flora's 'old man' really was; the only person who seems to fit in local burial records is a John Volckman, who died on 10th August 1900, aged 63. In his Will he bequeathed all his property to his sister Helen, and one of the few things Flora noted about 'Mr Foreshaw's' private life was that he had a sister.

Sir Frederick Pollock – One of the 'eminent men' who had come to live in the area, he was a lawyer. Instrumental in opening and naming the *Fox & Pelican* in Grayshott as a 'Refreshment House' in 1899. Shortly before his death in 1937, he advised on the form of Edward VIII's Abdication Act.

Arthur Conan Doyle – Needs little introduction. Flora does not name him in her book, but it can be no-one else! Came to live in Hindhead in 1897 for his wife's health, and had *Undershaw* built. Here he 'revived' Sherlock Holmes, and also became involved in local sporting activities. Described as 'a man with a hand that grips you heartily and, in its sincerity of welcome, hurts.' He served as a physician in the 2nd Boer War, and his pamphlet justifying Britain's action earned him a knighthood in 1902.

George Bernard Shaw – Had arrived in the area on honeymoon just before Flora arrived, and stayed for a couple of years more. In her book she tells us he was on a crutch (due to a fall from a bicycle) when she first sighted him, which helps us to date the occasion.

Bob Pikesley – Probably a composite of a number of small-holders whom Flora met in the Grayshott area. Many (but not all) of the facts she tells us about him correspond to one Albert Alderton who lived with his wife (not sister) in Whitmore Vale.

Winifred Storr – She lived 'up the road' in Hindhead. I found her diary in Haslemere Museum for the years 1898/99, written when she was 12. Her family was on familiar terms with Conan Doyle's and most of the other 'eminent' families of the area. She later married Gerald Brooke of Brooke Bond tea fame.

Grace ('Gee') Leuchars – Another real person, found in Winifred's diary. She was the daughter of an architect who lived in Grayshott village.

Marion – Worked in the sweet shop. I have no idea who she was.

Isobel ('Izzy') – The name of one of the 'garden of girls' mentioned by Flora in her book.

Richard Brownlow – Almost certainly William Burton Elwes who worked for Cable & Wireless during this period. He had joined the company in 1894 and retired, still a bachelor, on 30th March 1937 at the age of 59.

Mavis Brownlow – Almost certainly Lilian Bella Elwes. She married and had children, and I managed to contact a granddaughter of hers who verified Flora's description of 'my great-uncle Bill.' Interestingly, the story Flora tells us in her book about 'Mavis' contracting TB is not borne out in the Elwes family records – so either William made this up as an excuse for not seeing Flora again, or Flora made it up to save face with us the reader.

Mrs Parkhurst & Elsie – I needed the 1901 census to find 'Mrs Parkhurst.' She was in fact Alice Levett, who lived in *The Ferns*, The Avenue, Grayshott. It was the only house and family in the parish to fit Flora's description of it. Flora had left by that time and Mrs Levett had a different lodger. From the census, her 'Elsie' was in fact a boy, Aubrey! I can't believe Flora was that unobservant, so was she just altering the facts to protect her sources?

Mrs Davidson – Pure historical fact; the *Fox & Pelican* was indeed opened by the Bishop of Winchester's wife, though Flora doesn't tell us this. The Church of England was in favour of the establishment of 'Refreshment Houses' in place of Public Houses.

William Sillick – Flora mentions only a 'the reporter of a local newspaper.' He was almost certainly William Austen Sillick, who at the age of twenty-one was the sole local representative for the *Haslemere Herald* during the time that Flora was in Grayshott. He was an enthusiastic compiler of notes on the eminent people of the area. In Haslemere Museum, there is a lovingly gathered collection of newspaper cuttings and jottings of his, and a notebook in which he recorded information specifically about the personalities who lived in and around Grayshott. How ironic, then, that it includes no mention of the young girl he had walked with on the heaths, and sat with for hours by Waggoners Wells. But how could he have known then that, one day, she also would be worthy of a place in his collection? *Fittingly, in our first production the part was played by William Sillick's grandson.*

'Louie' Woods – I heard about 'Louie' from her daughter, who holds her mother's written memories of her time as a postwoman working with the Thompsons in Liphook.

John Thompson – 'Louie' Woods remembers John Thompson as a small, portly, well-dressed man with brown, wavy hair. He expected everyone to be as immaculately dressed as himself, with clean, neatly pressed uniform and shining brass buttons. He had a domineering personality and strong views, with the bearing and manner of a Sergeant-major. Everyone, she said, was in awe of him. However Eileen Leggett, who lived next door to the Thompsons in Griggs Green, said: "people think she was intimidated by him but, at least by the time I knew them, in her gentle way she managed him nicely." However there is little doubt that they were as different as chalk and cheese in their attitude to life in general.

Sergeant John Mumford – One soldier whom 'Louie' remembered in particular, according to her daughter, was a Sergeant John Mumford. Like several other men serving with Canadian regiments, including Flora's brother, Mumford was an Englishman by birth, born in Southend-on-Sea. Nevertheless we still played him with a Canadian accent! *I followed Sgt Mumford's army record and was glad to see that he survived the war and returned safely to Canada – in fact I have since corresponded with his great-grandson!*

Harry Envis – One of the postmen in Liphook mentioned by 'Louie' Woods. John Thompson's favourite relaxation was fishing. In his off-duty hours he would go with Harry Envis and others to Waggoners Wells or one of the other many ponds and lakes around Liphook.

'Joe' Leggett – He told me: "At the age of eight in 1916, I was interested to see what our new postmaster looked like and found an excuse to enter the post office to get a glimpse of him. It was some kind of poor excuse, and when I was asked what I wanted, I learned very quickly from Mr Thompson that the post office was not a place for little lads to spend their time." When the Thompsons bought their new house ten years later in 1926 he found he was their next-door neighbour!

Eileen Leggett – Eileen had a special reason to be grateful to Flora. "She decided there was no future for me working on the farm, yet there were few other openings in a little village like Liphook, whose population was then about 3,000 for the whole parish, so she suggested that I should apply for the post of part-time operator at the telephone exchange. I know I would not have been Mr Thompson's choice – but she arranged for me to get the appointment. So started two years or more of close association with Flora Thompson and her daughter."

Mrs Leggett – Talking of the time when they were next-door neighbours at Griggs Green, Eileen said: "We knew nothing of her being a writer, but my mother, a keen judge of character, soon decided that Mrs Thompson was a 'lady' but her husband 'no gentleman'."

Bill and Maggie Tidy – Flora tells us in her *Peverel Paper* of October 1925 about a tinker and his wife who 'made their home for forty years in the shelter of a circle of hollies.' John Budd in *Liphook Remembers* tells us more about them, including their name: Bill Tidy and his wife. The script draws from both these sources and the verbal memories of those in Liphook who remembered them well. I remember saying to Eileen Leggett at one of our performances that perhaps I'd gone a bit 'over the top' in writing their characters – "Oh no," she said, "they were far worse than that!"

145

Dr Ronald Campbell Macfie – A Scottish physician and writer who Flora first met in 1912 after she had won a competition to write a criticism on his ode about the sinking of the *Titanic*. From then on he became an inspiration to her writing. A friend summed him up as, 'a high strung breezy nature, loving much, fighting well, dreaming dreams and helping his fellow men, he was very gentle, very fierce, a devotee of beauty and a defender of the faith'. He was everything that John Thompson was not. When he died in 1931, Flora wrote his name on the fly-leaf of a book adding a quotation from Shakespeare's Cleopatra, 'The bright day is done and we are for the dark.'

Gypsy woman – The gypsy woman comes from *Peverel Papers*, November 1921, where Flora helps her to locate the wood-sage and is told: "You are goin' to be loved – loved by a lot o' folks – strangers shall become friends – people all over."

Winifred ('Diana') Thompson – Born October 1903 in Winton and named Winifred, but all her life she insisted on being called 'Diana.' She never married after her fiancé Cecil went to Australia with her brother Basil and stayed there. Eileen Leggett told me that she and Flora looked more like sisters than mother and daughter when walking around Liphook.

Basil Thompson – Born October 1909 in Winton. He is mentioned in the play but never seen.

Peter Thompson – Born 'unexpectedly' October 1918 in Liphook. 'Joe' Leggett told me he reminded them of Just William.

Sam the Shepherd – 'Joe' Leggett said: "In 1921 one of the farm cottages was made habitable for an old man who had helped on the farm; Flora Thompson loved to hear him speak of his earlier life as a shepherd and of his imaginary flock on Weavers Down – she would often bring him a tasty dish long before she came to live next to us." Much of my shepherd's text in the play is taken from Flora's observations in her *Peverel Papers*.

Appendix C – Staging considerations

The plays were written to be toured to unprepared venues such as village halls. As such they do not rely on stage scenery or theatrical lighting effects.

I was influenced by Keith Dewhurst's ideas of 'promenade' theatre which he used for the first performances of his own plays on Flora Thompson in the National Theatre. In this, the actors and audience share a space and there is no 'stage' as such – nor any seating except for the portable furniture used by the cast. No time is spent changing scenes – the action is continuous and 'scenes' develop in different parts of the auditorium to denote changes in location.

I wondered how this would work with typical local audiences and discussed this with Keith when I met him at a performance of his *Lark Rise* in Farnham, which was not performed 'in promenade'. He admitted that very few people tried it that way now due to reluctance or inability on the part of audiences to stand for that long.

Performance of Flora's Peverel at the Rural Life Centre, Tilford, 2007

*Harry Envis and 'Louie' Woods
with Mr Thompson*

Sam the Shepherd with Flora

My own experience echoes this. When we advertised a promenade performance the worried phone-calls began to arrive from locations chosen to host the play. Our first venue had received an enquiry from two Women's Institute parties, and were on the point of turning them away if we could not guarantee them seats. Our second venue was becoming equally concerned that a significant proportion of their clients were elderly and could not be expected to stand for two hours.

So we compromised. We still used the floor of the hall but put seats close to the acting area. The actors felt they were acting 'in the round' instead of in true 'promenade' but they could still communicate with the audience – and the shows went ahead.

By the same publisher – books relating to Flora Thompson

Heatherley, *by Flora Thompson*

This is the book which Flora Thompson wrote about her time in Grayshott. It is the 'missing' fourth part of her *Lark Rise to Candleford* collection in which 'Laura Goes Further'. Illustrated with chapter-heading line drawings.
  ISBN 978-1-873855-29-4 September 1998, notes, illustrations and maps.

The Peverel Papers, *by Flora Thompson*

Nature Notes written in Liphook, Hampshire, 1921–1927. Full unabridged version with notes and illustrations. *ISBN 978-1-873855-57-7 May 2008*

On the Trail of Flora Thompson—from Grayshott to Griggs Green, *by John Owen Smith*

The author has turned detective to discover the true identities behind the pseudonyms which Flora Thompson used for the local places and people she describes in *Heatherley*.
  ISBN 978-1-873855-24-9 First published May 1997, updated 2005.

Flora Thompson, the Story of the 'Lark Rise' Writer, *by Gillian Lindsay*

A full biography of Flora Thompson's life.
  ISBN 978-1-873855-53-9 Republished in updated form 2007.

Grayshott—the story of a Hampshire village, *by J. H. (Jack) Smith*

The history of Grayshott from its earliest beginnings as a minor hamlet of Headley to its status as a fully independent parish flourishing on (and across) the borders of Hampshire and Surrey.
  ISBN 978-1-873855-38-6 First published 1976, republished 2002

The Hilltop Writers—*a Victorian Colony among the Surrey Hills, by W.R. Trotter.* Rich in detail yet thoroughly readable, this book tells of sixty-six writers including Tennyson, Conan Doyle and Bernard Shaw who chose to work among the hills around Haslemere and Hindhead in the last decades of the 19th century. *ISBN 978-1-873855-31-7 March 2003, illustr. and maps.*

Also, from the Bramshott & Liphook Preservation Society:—

Guide to Liphook, Bramshott & neighbourhood (1925)—*mostly written by Flora Thompson*
Growing up in Griggs Green, *by Joe Leggett*
Flora's neighbour in Griggs Green writes of his memories.

John Owen Smith, publisher — www.johnowensmith.co.uk